MW00352174

Living in *Victory*

One Simple Prayer, One Miraculous
Rescue, and One Divine Destiny

Christel Novella

Trilogy Christian Publishers
A Wholly Owned Subsidiary of Trinity Broadcasting Network
2442 Michelle Drive
Tustin, CA 92780

Copyright © 2020 by Christel Novella

All Scripture quotations, unless otherwise noted, taken from THE HOLY BIBLE, NEW INTERNATIONAL VERSION®, NIV® Copyright © 1973, 1978, 1984, 2011 by Biblica, Inc.® Used by permission. All rights reserved worldwide.

Scripture quotations marked (KJV) taken from *The Holy Bible, King James Version.* Cambridge Edition: 1769.

All rights reserved, including the right to reproduce this book or portions thereof in any form whatsoever.

For information, address Trilogy Christian Publishing
Rights Department, 2442 Michelle Drive, Tustin, Ca 92780.
Trilogy Christian Publishing/ TBN and colophon are trademarks of Trinity Broadcasting Network.

For information about special discounts for bulk purchases, please contact Trilogy Christian Publishing.

Manufactured in the United States of America

Trilogy Disclaimer: The views and content expressed in this book are those of the author and may not necessarily reflect the views and doctrine of Trilogy Christian Publishing or the Trinity Broadcasting Network.

10 9 8 7 6 5 4 3 2 1

Library of Congress Cataloging-in-Publication Data is available.

ISBN 978-1-64088-221-8 (Print Book)
ISBN 978-1-64088-222-5 (ebook)

I waited patiently for the Lord;
he turned to me and heard my cry.

He lifted me out of the slimy pit,
out of the mud and mire;
he set my feet on a rock
and gave me a firm place to stand.

He put a new song in my mouth,
a hymn of praise to our God.
Many will see and fear the Lord
and put their trust in Him.
(Psalm 40:1–3, NIV)

First and foremost, I dedicate this book to Father God! Holy, holy is He!

To my Lord and Savior Jesus Christ, who was and is and is to come.

To the Holy Spirit, who was there with me in the darkest of days when I was all alone and not sure how to move forward. He was there comforting me, teaching me, and guiding me on the way I should go.

ACKNOWLEDGMENTS

I am thankful to my faithful mother, Helen Novella, and my courageous father, Giuseppe Novella, who didn't give up praying for me, as they watched their daughter sink into the pit of destruction.

I'm indebted to the leaders of Brookwood Church: Perry Duggar, Senior Pastor, for the opportunity and resources to film a testimony video and feature it during the Transformation sermon series. To David Hardy, Executive Pastor, and Marilyn Kendrick, Women's Ministry Director for encouraging and entrusting me to write this study for a group of women at Brookwood.

To my friend, Tina Moore, who reviewed and edited the study before it was presented to the church.

A special thanks to Meleah Allard, who edited my story into a shorter version for other media publications.

More thanks to my special sisters: Jill McNamara, a guiding light at the start of my journey. I will never forget attending my first Bible study at Brookwood and seeing the light of Jesus in her face and God directing me to follow her. To Tracy Palmer, who was with me in the trenches during some of the most trying and dark times, and gently guided me through the healing process. To Dee Barnes, my sister in ministry, for standing in truth, grace, and obedience to God. Her resolve enabled me to breakthrough many strongholds and find freedom and healing in Christ.

Thanks to my prayer partner, Tana Tuttle, who faithfully met with me and prayed with me weekly in South Carolina. Together, we saw wonderful things happen by God's hand, and now while I live in Florida, she continues to pray with me over the phone every Sunday.

I also thank, Cheryl Cannon, for her bold faith in Jesus and the power of the Holy Spirit, she is a tell-it-like-it-is-kind-of-girl with no fluff, and I *love* that. She's a major powerhouse in God's kingdom.

The Holy Spirit used Joyce Meyer as a virtual mentor to help me heal beautifully, especially using her show, *Enjoying Everyday Life*, and her book, *Battle Field of the Mind*. Her shows, books, DVDs, and CDs imparted truth to me exactly when I needed it, in an awe-inspiring way.

During the time Glenn Beck was on Fox News, I found him to be a man of truth, courage, and boldness. This inspired me to seek out truth, and I started reading my Bible again. Thank you, Glenn, for waking me up.

During some major attacks by the enemy, I found solace for my soul in praise and worship through the anointed music of Chris Tomlin that brought me to a place of victory. I especially love the song, *Thank You God For Saving Me*, which God has revealed to be my testimony song. And after sharing my testimony, my dream is to sing that song where God will set many others free at His appointed time.

ENDORSEMENTS

Christel has done a wondrous work in *Living in Victory* showing us what it looks like to step forward in faith, recognizing her sin needs of a Savior! You will relate as you read her story and sense her authentic heart and troubled spirit as she sought Him in the midst of her lifestyle choices. Christel so adeptly points us to God, asking us to recognize His voice, His words, and His presence in our midst. She will help you take that step to move forward in faith in the full acknowledgment of your sin and grasp the One who understands, who willingly paid the price for you! Her ability to point to the scriptures for our daily bread is tantamount to her story of faith walking while in the dark pit of sin, shame, and loneliness. What a joy it is to watch a sister in Christ boldly claim her faith and position in His kingdom, fitting for His people in a fallen world!

May we all feel the freedom that Christel so beautifully shines in her testimony, life, and work. A resounding hallelujah for this work and testimony!

—Jill McNamara, Dallas Theological Seminary
master student, one of Christel's biggest
fans, as well as her sister in Christ

Living in Victory walks the reader through the practical steps of what it means to put obedience to God above all else. Through her powerful personal testimony, Christel Novella shares the struggles and victories she has faced as God called her to walk away from the accepted cultural norms of today in order to embrace the life He has called her to live. Her transparency with others is both refreshing and encouraging. This study asks its readers some challenging questions while pointing them straight to the One who has all the answers!

—Stephanie Baker, clinical pastoral counselor,
founder, and president of Life in Abundance

Living in Victory by Christel Novella is filled with personal determination, God's blessings, and scriptural insight. It's a callback to God and His Word. It's a bold application for the reader—scattered with real, honest life moments shared by the author. It's a bold, thought-provoking, and interactive—a must-read for the Christian who desires to live in God's best over the distractions and temptations so readily available in today's world.

—Sandy Bowers, owner and graphic
designer for WindUp Creative

Most people love a good story, but not all stories point to the Author of Life, Jesus Christ. Living in Victory not only brings readers to Jesus through Christel's story, but most importantly to the Word of God, which contains the most important story of all time: how Jesus Christ has come to rescue us from sin and set us on a firm foundation of grace, forgiveness and new life through himself. This study will show each of us how we all really are, much more alike than different: needy of transformation through the gospel. Dig in, and stay in this study to the end, trusting that God will "bring you into a spacious place" (Psalm 18:19) of freedom in Christ.

—Ellen Mary Dykas, Bible teacher / author
Sexual Sanity for Women: Healing from
Sexual and Relational Brokenness

First, I count it an honor to be chosen for acknowledging Christel and her book Living in Victory. The title sums up Christel's latest chapter in life, one of victory. This book is full of faith building testimony and scriptures you can stand on. Christel chose the narrow way which is victory in Him over darkness. Let this book and the Holy Spirit guide you to the victory won at Calvary.

—Ben Edwards, Follower of Christ

Christel's openness and honesty of her personal struggles is heart warming. Her desire to help others find freedom is precious. This book will encourage the reader to ask themselves the hard but life changing questions. The Word tells us we shall know the truth and the truth will set us free. Thank you Christel for sharing the story of your journey of finding The Truth, The Way and The Life and the freedom that has followed.

—Cheryl Cannon, Sister in Christ

CONTENTS

FOREWORD

What a tremendous delight and privilege to witness Christel Novella's journey from a frontline view, up front and personal… right by her side!

I met Christel the very day she decided to open up about her story for the first time. I knew our meeting was purposed—an appointed day and time that I had "stumbled upon." However, I had no idea what a wild ride we had just boarded and all that would unfold in the following three years.

I've had the opportunity to walk with many women through their healing. But one thing I knew from the start was that Christel was different…handpicked, called, and plucked from the pit for God's purposes for this day and time. She is a unique personality. Strong. Gifted. She's a powerhouse that God planned to deliver from darkness to the kingdom of light in short order. I sensed that her particular calling required being thrown in the proverbial deep end to mature quickly. And God did not disappoint.

Christel seemed to liken Paul in that she had been "all that and a bag of chips" in the world's eyes—a self-made woman living the high life and writing her own rules. Once she submitted to her road to Tarsus, her "come to Jesus" surrender, she would be pruned deeply and stripped of all that she thought she was.

While Christel had me at her side and many great friends, teachers, divine appointments, and resources, God really took Christel under His very own wing. Holy Spirit discipled her as she poured for hours through the Word looking for *truth*, digging, eating, and applying each revelation to the day at hand.

As our Father God is, He was gentle with her, carefully peeling the layers as she could handle it. There were joyous victories and heart-ripping, hard-fought battles. God

> I will lead her into the desert and speak tenderly to her there. I will return her vineyards to her and transform the Valley of Trouble into a gateway of HOPE. She will give herself to me there, as she did long ago when she was young.
> (Hosea 2:14–15)

faithfully brought her out the other side.

This Bible study is like a treasure map. In it, you will discover the path that God carved out in His Word day by day to free His daughter, rewrite her thinking, and reveal to her true identity.

Tracy E. Palmer, Cofounder Dance of Marriage Ministry

PREFACE

It all started with a simple prayer to God to take me out of the *pit* of the homosexual lifestyle of over twenty years. God answered my prayer with some devastating news and an encounter with Him that would *forever* change my life. Not knowing what to do or whom to turn to, God ushered in the Holy Spirit to take me through a beautiful process—intimacy with the Father, learning my identity in Christ, and the process to wholeness.

This book tells my story of how God answered my simple prayer: "Help me, Jesus. Help me." What I saw was a mountain in front of me, knowing there was no way in my power I could do what He was asking me to do, but then God revealed to me that my part was the act of obedience and that He would take it from there. He reminded me about the story of Abraham and what He asked him to do to test his faith, and I felt like this was my test. He would let me know the timing to move, and then on His cue, I would put one foot in front of the other and open my mouth, and He would fill it. Once that act of obedience was complete, God moved in *all* of His power to do the heavy lifting. My story is filled with miracles of how God moved in such a mighty way and how He tested my faith. I felt a sense from the Holy Spirit that He had major plans for my life but needed even more testing to see if I was up for the call.

My Bible study is the beautiful process the Holy Spirit took me through. I knew God would have me deliver this process as a Bible study, so I said yes and would wait for an open door. I thoroughly enjoyed attending the women's group WOW (Women of the Word) at my church, Brookwood. I developed much knowledge, wisdom, and insight as we studied the Lifeway Bible Studies. I went through several years learning, growing, and thriving in this beautiful community of women believers. I eventually started coleading some of the studies. Then one summer, they asked me to lead and then asked me a very unusual question: "Have you ever thought about writing a study?" Well, I knew this was God opening the door for me to deliver and write this study. The Holy Spirit would wake me up around 3:00 a.m. or 4:00 a.m., and I would start writing. It was as though a river of life was flowing through me as I typed away.

It was a major experience delivering this study to a group of women as I watched God work in their lives. Even though God brought me out of a life of homosexuality, the process to healing and experiencing complete wholeness is the *same*! It's all about knowing who we are as God's loved, chosen, and holy people (see Colossians 3:12) and then living in that identity. So no matter what area of struggle or past wounds you may be carrying, this study will help you on your journey to wholeness in Christ. Below is a testimony from one of my Bible study participants.

It has been such a joy to have Christel walk alongside me as I matured in my newfound relationship and freedom in Christ. She has been a great source of encouragement, prayer and inspiration. In her study, Living in Victory, she focuses on true surrender and repentance, being obedient and trusting God's call on your life through the genuineness of her own struggles. I was challenged daily to read and meditate on scripture. She provides many resources to keep you connected and digging in to Jesus. This study has been a strategic tool leaving me prepared for battle and to live in ultimate victory! (Lorena Collins from Greenville, South Carolina)

I knew in my spirit that God wanted me to share His story of transformation and healing with others on a larger scale. He put it on my heart that I would publish it in the future but to wait on Him again for the cue to move forward. It wasn't until 2018, four years later after delivering the Bible study, that I got the notion the timing was getting close. Then in October of 2018, I saw an advertisement about Trilogy, TBN's new publishing division, and then got the cue from the Holy Spirit to move forward in the process, and so here I am as a brand-new author with a story from God that will fulfill my testimony verse above: "Many will see and fear and will trust confidently in the Lord."

I pray the Lord meets you in a mighty way as you read my story and work through this Bible study.

We are in a battle for this generation, and God has called me to the frontlines to be a voice of His truth in a society fueled by deception.

INTRODUCTION

Living in Victory is a seven-week Bible study that will take you on a personal journey to help you understand where you are in your own walk with the Lord and develop a closer relationship with Him. You may feel stuck or wonder why you have no direction. You may have a struggle in your life and wonder why you can't break free from it. You may be in a crisis and don't have the strength to move forward. I believe with the direction and help of the Holy Spirit, this study will open your eyes, fill your heart, and provide God's power to remove all obstacles for a clear path to find God's abundant plan for your life.

You may ask, what authority do I have to help you in your walk with the Lord? Well, according to the world's standards, *none*. I don't have a counseling or theology degree, but what I do have is the best teacher in the universe: the Holy Spirit. In 2011, God gave me a *wake-up call to repentance*. I was saved at twelve but, in my early twenties, allowed the world to rule my life; so I kept sliding deeper and deeper into the *pit* (Satan's trap). Then a crisis hit my life that I had no control over, but I knew who did. I started seeking God for an answer, and He gave me two choices: life or death—turn from your current sinful lifestyle, and I will bless you; or stay on this path and choose death? I chose life but knew I couldn't do it on my own strength, so I gave it to God and asked Him to help me to be obedient to His call. Each day was extremely difficult, but God took me by the hand and led me step by step. When I gave it all to God, He reached down and pulled me out of that pit. He did all the heavy lifting, but I had to let go and truly give it to Him. It was the most powerful encounter I had ever experienced. My family couldn't believe the change, and my mom will tell you it was a true miracle.

This study coincides with the miraculous transformational power of God's grace as He took me by the hand, leading me to walk step by step in faith, into complete victory in the Lord Jesus Christ. My life is not perfect by any means, but what I can say is that I used to know about God and Jesus, and now I truly *know* Him. It's a relationship that is priceless. However, a relationship has two parts. God will give you all the grace you need, but you have to do your part. You have to be obedient to His Word and His calling on your life. You have to give Him priority in your life, or you will never find the amazing and abundant life He has in store for you. You will seek me and find me when you seek me with all your heart (Jeremiah 29:13). You may ask, how long will it take for me to know His plan? Well, that is different for everyone, and the pace is up to you. The more you put Him first and are obedient to His Word, the faster you will move on to the next level He has for you on your journey from glory to glory. However, He won't require too much too soon, just a little at a time. He will test your faith, and what is cool about God is that He will never fail you. He will allow you to take the test over and over again until you pass.

If you are ready to do what it takes and want to experience true victory and the power of God in your life, then I encourage you to put this study as a priority into your schedule.

Living in Victory saying: "Holy Spirit, think through me, live through me, and love through me" (Sarah Young, *Dear Jesus*).

Victory Verses

For the Lord takes delight in his people; he crowns the humble with victory. (Psalm 149:4 NIV)

But thanks be to God! He gives us the *victory* through our Lord Jesus Christ. (1 Corinthians 15:57 NIV)

For everyone born of God overcomes the world. This is the *victory* that has overcome the world, even our faith. (1 John 5:4 NIV)

And we know that all things work together for good to them that love God, to them who are the called according to his purpose. (Romans 8:28 KJV)

A Wake-Up Call to Repentance and the Journey to Freedom

During an intimate time with the Lord one morning, He highlighted the verse below as my testimony verse. It was a very powerful moment of surrender, revelation, and freedom that I will carry with me for the rest of my life. I know that only through Him can I be set free. This verse is the catalyst that would drive me to share my story to help others experience the glory, the *love*, and the power of God in a life that is completely surrendered to the Lord.

> I waited patiently for the Lord;
> he turned to me and heard my cry.
> He lifted me out of the slimy pit,
> out of the mud and mire;
> he set my feet on a rock
> and gave me a firm place to stand.
> He put a new song in my mouth,
> a hymn of praise to our God.
> Many will see and fear the Lord
> and put their trust in him. (Psalm 40:1–3)

God showed me that until I completely "let go and let God" (completely surrender my will), then He will draw close and release His power into a life who is willing to follow Him. We must depend on Him for every decision that affects our path. He wants us to make Him the priority over everything else. He wants us to believe in His Word and do what it says. Once we believe this and *live it*, then we can experience victory in our lives. Now I am not saying there won't be hard times, but we can have victory even in those times when we truly learn how to lean on Him.

My Testimony

I grew up in a middle-class Italian-Catholic family in New Jersey. My dad owned his own business and worked a lot like most fathers. He did very well, so we were not lacking in the material realm. Mom worked at home in the business home office, so she was always home with my younger brother and me. Life was good.

Mom began a personal search for truth, and we started attending different churches. One of my mom's friends invited us to her church. When the Gospel was preached, I responded and became a born-again Christian at the age of twelve. My entire family became believers around the same time. We eventually ended up in a church that we all loved. I had a wonderful youth pastor and youth group that helped me grow and get close to God. I was on fire for Him and started serving and sharing the Gospel with others.

Once I hit 16 and began dating, I met a cute guy at a Christian rollerskating church event. We became physical and my relationship with God took a backseat. No one told me about the battles and temptations I would face as a teenager and how to overcome them through the spiritual weapons at our disposal: God's Word, prayer, thanksgiving, praise, and worship.

Sure, I went to church and Sunday school and Wednesday night prayer meeting, and that was good for a while…so what was missing? Thinking back on a few things that could have been missing in my walk. First, understanding that we are in a spiritual war and that God has provided the weapons to fight this battle (2 Corinthians 10:4). Second, the true meaning of the hymn "I Surrender All"? What are we surrendering? Our will for His will. I thought we had to do everything on our own. I thought as long as we read the Bible and attended church, we were good to go.

At seventeen, I worked at an Italian pizza restaurant. I was in such rebellion that I left the house to live with a girl from work and her two kids. I remember the day I was moving in her husband was moving out. I didn't even tell my parents where I was. They were worried sick.

Eventually, I moved out and into an apartment with my boyfriend who I met at the restaurant. He had a brother who abused his wife both verbally and physically, and when I saw the first indication of the physical abuse in my boyfriend, I, at least, was smart enough to leave that situation. However, the decision to live with and engage sexually with my boyfriend was not without its consequences. I wound up getting pregnant and had an abortion without any remorse. So sad now looking back at my callous attitude as the decision was based on removing an inconvenience and not killing a precious life from God. God would bring this decision to the forefront much later in my healing process to finally allow me to experience much shame, grief, and repentance that would bring about a complete restoration and healing in my soul. That story could be a book in and of itself.

An Enlightening Encounter at the Bar

At eighteen, I was in complete party mode when I started working at a restaurant called Bennigan's. It was a restaurant by day and a club by night. But then one night, God opened my eyes and removed the veil of this "glorious" lifestyle and allowed me to see it with spiritual eyes. I will never forget it. I got off work early and sat with some friends at a table near the dance floor, specifically with my best friend's boyfriend and his friends as we waited for my girlfriend to get off work. I remember looking all around me as if everything was in slow motion—people talking, talking loud all around me, laughing, red lights flashing, and smoke rising from the dance floor as if I had a glimpse into hell. A man at the bar, drunk off his gourd, couldn't even pick up his head.

I remember God speaking to my heart, saying, *That man will be you if you keep on going in the direction you are headed.* Then everything stopped as my friend's boyfriend asked me a question. He said, "Maybe one night when my girlfriend is working, we can get together." *Really!* I thought. I looked at him with eyes wide open and said, "You are worthless," and I walked out of the restaurant. As I was walking out, I experienced a whole new perspective for my destiny. I knew that I didn't want any part of this crazy, sinful life of drinking, partying, drugs, and sex. Looking back, I realized that God used that moment to show me what this world has to offer: emptiness, worthlessness, deception, and a road that leads to spiritual and physical destruction.

I started reading my Bible and going back to church. I could feel the presence of God coming back into my life. I decided I wanted to do something with my life, so I started praying, and God directed me into nursing at a university in Greenville, South Carolina.

The Rug Pulled out from under My Feet

During my first year in college, I met a friend from Canada, and we really hit it off and spent all our extra time together. We would walk to class together and meet for lunch. We were inseparable. Little did I know the devil was going to use her to pull the spiritual rug right out from under my feet, and I fell flat into homosexuality. After we became intimate, I felt like something evil had invaded my body. I felt like a zombie walking around campus. I couldn't eat or sleep for over a week. People would ask me, "What is wrong with you?" I am not sure how I ever answered that question. However, looking back my thought was I sinned against my own body. (1 Corinthians 6:18). I had fallen to sexual sin in the past and could suppress those feelings of desire and eventually end the relationships but *not* with this sin: the *sin* of homosexuality. The feeling and attraction for this relationship was so strong that I didn't do anything to leave it or run from it. After the first semester, we moved off campus together and became a secret couple. We were together during my entire college season.

I started feeling very guilty about my lifestyle. I started to attend a Baptist church nearby and was no longer having an intimate relationship with my partner. She eventually found someone else, and we broke up. Now I was free, or so I thought, but didn't realize this wasn't something that just goes away. I started having an attraction to the girl that my partner first dated after we broke up. This attraction became so strong that I started to pursue her, and we eventually got together for dinner.

Well, as the story goes, that was all she wrote. We hit it off and started a relationship. I owned a small house, and she lived in an apartment, so she moved in with me. We had tons of fun and enjoyed each other's company. As the Bible says, sin can be fun for a season but eventually catches up with us as the *convic-*

tion of the Holy Spirit wells up inside on those who are born again. After five years or so, I remember sitting in my office with such conviction that I decided to just go into the living room and let her know that I couldn't do this anymore. So I did, and she was devastated. She got up and left, but I was so *sad* and didn't want to live without my best friend. I just couldn't do this on my own. I called her and told her I was sorry and that I didn't want to live without her. She came back with much hesitation and hurt. My flesh was happy, but my soul was empty and longing for God, the only one who could fill my void. So we got back together, and it took years for her to feel secure in our relationship again.

The Wake-Up Call

Then thirteen years into our relationship, a very small spot was noted on a routine X-ray in the left lower lobe of her lungs. The doctor wanted to remove it, so surgery was scheduled. It was positive for cancer, so he removed the lobe immediately. He said they got it very early and didn't note any other spots, so there was no need for any further treatment. We were elated!

Then eighteen years into our relationship, several spots were found in several of her lobes. The doctor scheduled more surgery and tried to remove them all, but one was in an area that was too risky to remove. Talk about chemotherapy was now underway, and we both realized this story didn't have a happy ending.

During this ordeal of months with doctors and tests, I was feeling powerless and knew there was only one person who could help us. I felt the nudging of the Holy Spirit. I started watching the news instead of all the fantasy shows we used to watch together. The news was the only *truth* I had in my life. I started watching Glenn Beck. He would talk about how God was working in his life. He talked about reading the Bible. I started reading the Bible and praying for my partner. I asked God to forgive me for my lifestyle because I knew the entire time I was in the relationship that it was *wrong*. My friends would ask me if I believed homosexuality is a sin, and I would be upfront with them and say, "Yes, I believe it is a *sin* and is *wrong*," but I didn't know how I could leave my best friend. I was putting my friend before God.

Who changed the truth of God into a lie, and worshipped and served the creature more than the Creator, who is blessed for ever. Amen. (Romans 1:25)

So here I am, reading my Bible and praying as I watch Glenn Beck every day on Fox News at 5:00 p.m. I couldn't wait until 5:00 p.m. every weekday to get some truth about our country and the condition of our society. I actually started becoming interested in politics for the first time.

Then one day, I received a postcard in the mail from a church called Brookwood. I left it on the kitchen counter and felt led to visit. I will never forget one statement on the card: "Come as you are." I started to cry as I couldn't believe a church would want a sinner like me to darken their doors. I asked my partner (who I will now refer to as J) if she wanted to go, and she agreed. I couldn't believe it. Maybe the Lord would bring us both to Himself. So we attended our first day at Brookwood. We read the sign to put on our flashers if we were first-time visitors, so we did. We were escorted into the building to the welcome booth. We looked up into the massive atrium and couldn't believe the size of the church. It reminded me of a concourse in an airport. Come to find out that is what they called that part of the building. It even had a bookstore on the second floor, so we checked it out after the service. We noticed a small devotional book called *Jesus Is Calling*. So we bought it, and J read it every morning. I was so encouraged! We also noticed another book called *Coming Out of Homosexuality*, and I remember J saying, "I hope they don't go there, or I am out of here." She knew at that time where I stood on the subject, but I don't think she ever wanted to believe it.

Last Call to Choose Life or Death

After reading the Bible and praying for weeks, I had a divine encounter where God spoke to my heart, and it was *very* clear. He said, *It is time for you to turn from your life of sin. If you do, I will bless you and her. If you don't, it is death for the both of you.* And I believe that "death" was a spiritual death and a physical death. I medicated myself so much by this time, drinking, smoking cigarettes and pot that I started to feel very unhealthy. I started having heartburn and reflux every night. I even started having some slight chest pain. After I

I call heaven and earth as witnesses today against you, that I have set before you life and death, blessings and cursing; therefore choose life, that both you and your descendants may live; that you may love the LORD your God, that you may obey His voice, and that you may cling to Him, for He is your life and the length of your days; and that you may dwell in the land of the LORD swore to your fathers, to Abraham, Isaac, and Jacob, to give them. (Deuteronomy 30:19–20) encountered God's clear instruction, I remember crying so hard and looking up to heaven with tears streaming down my face and saying, "There is no way I can do this to my best friend during this critical time in her life. You are going to have to do it!" My prayer was very simple:

"Help me, Jesus. Help me!"

I gave it *all* over to God and He gave me the faith and knowing that He would do all the heavy lifting but I had to put my part into *action*: I prayed every day for hours and read my Bible. I would cry myself to sleep. God would give me enough strength to get through one day at a time. Now my prayer was, *God, when do I tell her?*

Everything around me seemed like it was crashing down. I left my corporate sales job in December of 2009. I had started my own marketing company in 2007, so I decided to go full-time on my own. I was on Cobra for a while until the hospital system where J worked allowed same-sex partners to have insurance. However, my insurance card would have her name on it and not mine. We had to reapply for that insurance by the end of September 2011, which entailed an office visit to get my blood work done. I felt a check in my spirit as I realized that the moment I hand the receptionist my insurance card, I was declaring our homosexual relationship legally and publicly.

I went ahead and got my labs done and had to wait on the results to complete the paperwork. During this time, J was on her third chemo treatment. I was petrified and very anxious and wondered every day, *Is this the day, Lord, that you want me to tell her?* I felt all alone and didn't have anyone to talk to. I remember when I was twelve that my family listened to Charles Stanley, so I looked him up online. I decided I would send him a letter and ask him for the best timing to confront her. I have to say, I was quite distraught while writing this letter. Here is part of that letter:

> *I just don't know when to do it.* Should I do it when she is sick and throwing up, wait until she is better and has a stronger will to fight, or wait for the lab results to come back, etc.? *How will I know when God wants me to do this?* I know she will get angry, and I guess I am afraid that she will stop seeking God. I also know when we obey God, things work out better. I hope God will save her and possibly heal her because of my obedience.
>
> I also asked God for a sign similar to your "two shooting stars" request (this was a sign that Charles Stanley had requested from God for confirmation). J got a plant when she was in the hospital, and it almost died. I replanted it to a new pot and water it regularly. It was almost dead with its leaves shriveled up and brown, but there was a slight bit of green left, so I asked God to revive the plant to show me if He is going to save her soul. That is my main prayer every day: that God will open J's heart and eyes to His love and truth and give her a desire to read his Word, follow Him, and ask Christ to be her Savior.

I never received a response to my e-mail. However, looking back, God had me write this letter to record that moment in time as a record for my testimony.

The Pot Roast Experience

I believe with all my heart that this was my last call for repentance as I had grieved the Holy Spirit for so long, that when God asked me to turn from my sinful lifestyle, it was clear that He was asking me to choose between life or death. I could feel the spirit of death on me and working in my life. It was a slow progression of bad habits and my sinful lifestyle that were finally catching up with me. *But* God gave me an encounter that would answer another prayer and keep me on course toward choosing life.

I was having guests over at the house, and I remember being very apprehensive about this gathering as it was during the time when I was still waiting on God to give me the timing to tell J we had to break our sinful ties. I guess I was concerned about their influence on me with this newfound truth bubbling inside that I wanted to protect. I prayed and prayed before they came over for the "devil to be left at the door," not sure why I used those specific words, but I kept praying that over and over for the devil to be left at the door. So what happened was not at all what I had expected.

I was making a roast for dinner, and after they arrived and where gathering outside around the pool, I decided to taste the roast to see if it was done. I was so hungry that I cut a large piece and didn't chew it very well, so it got stuck and lodged in my esophagus. I tried drinking water to make it go down, but the water would come right back up. J tried the Heimlich maneuver multiple times but nothing worked. J got on the phone with the doctor, and we tried everything to get it to go down.

I was foaming at the mouth and felt like I was having a heart attack. So after a few hours, J took me to the emergency room at the main hospital. I remember getting to the hospital holding my hand over my heart and could barely speak as the pain was excruciating! They immediately put me in a wheel chair and wheeled me off to a room. They hooked me up to the monitors and started an IV. I remember laying in the hospital bed waiting for what seemed like an eternity for the nurse to bring some pain medicine. Then everything stopped as in slow motion as I took in my surroundings (sound familiar). Then I heard the Lord say these words in my heart, *This is the beginning of what death looks like.* An awakening in my soul happened immediately as the fear of the Lord set my mind and will to stay the course of obedience.

After a few more hours of tests, blood work, and finally some sedation, they came and took me into the operating room.

The doctor asked me, "Chicken or steak?"

And I replied, "Roast." I smiled and laughed and was feeling some relief from the sedation at that time. The procedure was quick and painless as I was asleep during the process. I remember waking up with much relief and such peace that God was with me during the entire ordeal. What a wild way to answer my prayer, but God's ways are not our ways. He answered my prayer with another wake-up call. We think that when we go through suffering that it's a bad thing, but in actuality, it's what forces us to stop, look up and seek God's voice among all the distractions.

Now Is the Time to Tell Her

Then the day came. It was triggered by a health insurance letter for the self-employed as God had stickily given me the directive to not renew the hospital's same-sex health insurance program with J. Once I opened the letter and read the benefits, I knew this was a perfect fit for me. Then everything stopped with a moment of pause where I heard the Lord say in my heart,

"Now is the time, and I will take care of your insurance." When I knew it was the time, I just stood there frozen and felt the Holy Spirit say, *Just put one foot in front of the other and go to J and open your mouth, and I will fill it.* So I put one foot in front of the other into the room where I opened my mouth and told J that I couldn't be on her insurance and why. I told her with tears streaming down my face. I told her that I could no longer live in this lifestyle but would still take care of her as a friend. She was devastated and almost fell on the floor. I can't even remember what happened after that moment, but it was the hardest thing I ever had to do in my life. As days went by, we still slept in the same bed. We would watch TV, and I would comfort her at night as she was going through her chemo treatments. After her fourth round of chemo, they gave her a break; and after two weeks, she started feeling better.

I knew God wanted me to move upstairs to the guest bedroom, and that conviction kept getting stronger. I prayed about it and asked Him to show me when and I would do it. Then I remember, in the middle of the night, one of the smoke alarms starting to go off due to a low battery. My legs started cramping so I had to move to the couch so not to disturb J. That night, I felt like God was trying to get my attention, and He was answering my question on when to move upstairs: *now*. I think moving to the upstairs bedroom was the most difficult move in the process as it was the finalizing factor and realization that we were no longer a "couple."

The enemy was strong, but God showed me He was much stronger if I relied on Him. I remember days of being confronted and persecuted by J, and God would give me the words. I didn't even know what I was saying and would think back on the conversation and see how the Lord guided the conversation. A lesbian friend of ours told me about a lady, Joyce Meyer, and I started watching and recording her shows. God was using every show to guide me along the way in His truth during my entire process. She taught about spiritual warfare, and then a friend of mine lent me her book, *Battle Field of the Mind*, so I made sure to put on my armor every morning to confront whatever attack may be on the horizon.

J started doing really well as the treatments were working to keep the cancer at bay. The green plant started growing a few new leaves. God was showing me that He would keep His promise.

I started attending Brookwood Church on a regular basis and volunteered in the production team. I found it fascinating and loved it. I joined the women's group WOW and started attending the powerful bible studies. Day by day, I grew stronger in the Lord knowing He was with me.

J could see the change in me, and I think it scared her. Then one day she looked at me and said, "I don't know who you are anymore, and I want to move out." So God put it in her heart to leave. I knew in my heart that I would never ask her to leave and that I would take care of her as long as she would let me, but I couldn't be in that lifestyle if God was going to bless us.

So now we needed to figure out how to get her name off the mortgage so she could buy her own place. During this time, my business wasn't doing very well due to my personal circumstances and wondered how I could possibly refinance the mortgage in my name. I called the mortgage company, and when they asked for my earnings, I told them the truth. They said there was no way I could refinance the house on those numbers. I told J, and we tried to figure out what to do so she could get her own place. So I prayed about it, and then here comes that pause again as I felt the Lord ask me to *give Him everything*, even the house. The Holy Spirit gave me this knowing inside that I was being tested to completely surrender *all* for the call that is on my life. So I decided to obey and put the house up for sale on Zillow. I took pictures and listed it myself. However, not one e-mail or interest came in for over two months. I called the mortgage company for the second time, hoping we could figure something out. No go! I just didn't have the income. J was getting frustrated, and so I decided to get serious and ask a realtor that I knew who could get the job done.

I met with her on April 16, Monday, at 10:00 a.m. She didn't list the house at that time but wanted to get the house professionally staged, so I met with the stager on Tuesday. I shared my story with both women who are believers and would understand my situation. God used them to encourage me during this time of trial. The thought of getting the house ready for staging was so overwhelming that I procrastinated. Finally, on Monday, April 23, I decided to get serious and started working on boxing stuff up.

God Sends an Angel and Performs a Miracle

On Tuesday morning, I got the very first e-mail from Zillow. The contact in the email asked if I would consider leasing the house for two years. I thought maybe this is a way I can keep the house. So I called my realtor to find out if she had any ideas where leasing the house would release J from the mortgage. She suggested I call the mortgage company. So this was my third time calling the mortgage company to determine my options to release J from the mortgage. I got on my knees with hands folded in prayer on my office chair, and I prayed for God to send me the right person to talk to. I got on the phone, and the lady on the other end answered, "Hello, this is Angel. How can I help you?" At that moment, I knew the Lord was going to work a miracle. I found out that Angel was a Christian, so I told her my story and asked if a lease could make a difference in keeping the house. She said that it didn't. I asked her about my options to keep the house and release J from the mortgage. We talked about having a cosigner, and my brother came to mind immediately. She suggested that I ask him. I could tell that she really wanted to help me. Thanks, Lord, for sending me an angel! So I called my brother and could barely get out the words without crying during the entire conversation. He said he would cosign the loan with me. I started to cry; I just couldn't believe it. I said that he needed to ask Terry, his wife, and we also decided that I should ask Dad to give him the first option to be the cosigner. I called Dad, and he said he would cosign. *Wow!*

Then I called Angel back, and she was really excited. She also started asking me more questions about my past income. I let her know that I didn't make much in 2011, but my CPA had to file an extension on my taxes. She stopped me right there and said, "So you haven't filed your taxes for 2011?" I said I hadn't and that this was a first for me. She then asked me for income figures three years prior, so I gave her those numbers. I could hear her clicking away on the calculator keys, and then she stopped and said to me, "Since you filed an extension and you have decent income in the three years prior, we can refinance your loan, and you *don't* need a cosigner." *What!* Then God gave me the icing on the cake. I got an appraisal for free, a low interest rate at 4 percent with no points, a check for $1,000 from escrow, and a month off from any payments. The new payment was $400 lower than the first mortgage. Thank You, Lord! She said I would hear from the processor in three to five days if they had any questions.

The loan took a little longer than expected, but we finally closed in God's timing. J found a house, and she closed on it on our anniversary, and she moved out on her dad's birthday. This process taught me that God is very specific in His timing.

So we lived in the house for a year together before J left, but God was faithful and got me through each day and gave me Joyce to uplift and fill me with His truth and wisdom. I let J know that she could take whatever she wanted, and she was very fair with her selections, and the whole process of separating our stuff went very smoothly. God did all the heavy lifting; I just had to obey Him and have faith. He did it all.

Do You Think You Were Saved during All These Years Living in Sin?

People ask me, "Do you believe you were saved during all those years of living in sin?" And I can say, "Yes, I know that I was saved the entire time."

How can I say that with such assurance? First, because God gives us assurance when we accept Jesus as Savior. The Holy Spirit comes and resides in our hearts. It is a supernatural experience and presence that is very hard to describe in words. It's an internal knowing that you are connected to God. What is so reassuring about our salvation is that God is filled with so much mercy and grace that no matter how far we run from Him, He is always there waiting for us to return to Him with open arms. However, I do believe there comes a time when God gives us a last call for repentance or deal

This day I call the heavens and the earth as witnesses against you that I have set before you life and death, blessings and curses. Now choose life, so that you and your children may live. (Deuteronomy 30:19)

with the severe consequences (Deuteronomy 30:15–20); this is clearly what happened to me the night He called me to repentance. The second reason I had assurance of my salvation was the *conviction* in my heart from the Holy Spirit. I would suppress that conviction by striving for the things of this world, thinking they could provide the satisfaction I was longing for and it may have for a season. But then all that wears off, and you are still left with a void that only one thing can truly fill—Jesus Christ. He created us with that void, and until we find Him, nothing will ever fill it—not fame, wealth, power, or pleasure. We'll always want more.

God Gave Me Assurance of His Promise on Easter

As I look back on my life, I can see God's presence, especially around Easter time. This first Easter by myself was such a *joy*. God put J on my heart on May 26, 2013, after she had been in her new house for about eight months. I sent her a text that said, "Hi, J, encouraging news about a miracle cancer drug that can kill every form of cancer. Still in testing but sounds very promising. I posted it on FB this morning. God has given me complete confidence that He is going to fulfill His promise to me about blessing *you*! God bless you and have a wondrous Easter!" Then she texted me back, "Good to hear…getting my PET scan in a few minutes…have to cut off my phone. Thanks for letting me know." God had me text her right before her PET scan to remind her of His promise and show me that He was going to keep it.

Her doctor also came to her shortly after this test to let her know that she had a rare gene that no one else in her entire practice had and that she no longer had to take IV chemo but could take a pill. The doctor was very encouraged by this new treatment.

We texted again in December 2013, where she shared some positive results from the latest PET scans showing no further growth of the cancer and the doctors reduced her dose on the pill in half. I was filled with so much *joy* as I watched God move on her behalf.

By the way, the green plant is flourishing and may need a new pot soon.

Call into Ministry

By January 2014, I had been living off my savings and some business income during my transformation process, which had allowed me to develop a close relationship with God. I considered that to be one of the best investments I have ever made. I am very driven, so I thought, *I really need to up my business income.* However, every time I wanted to advertise my business, God would always put ministry work in my path and let me know He was God and would supply my needs. During this time, He had been molding my heart for full-time ministry. I tried to run from it, but He kept bringing me back with divine appointments to make it very clear where He wanted me. I could write another two pages on how this all came about. So I deposited the last of my savings, walked out of the bank, and looked up and said, "I trust You, Lord."

At that moment, I had a text come in from a ministry leader that wanted to skype with me to ask me a question. He had never asked me to skype before, so I knew this was important. So I went home and got on Skype, and he asked me to come on board as their media manager. He asked me to pray about it, but I let him know, as in the past, his timing was a divine answer, as I already knew in my heart this was where God wanted me. Then he informed me that I would need to raise support and trust God in the beginning for my income. *Wow*, this mountain looked steep, but God had been with me through all of this, so I would continue to trust Him to supply as He promises when we obey Him.

On May 2, 2014, J posted on Facebook that she just completed a routine PET scan that was 100 percent clear and they were taking her off the chemo pill and would do a repeat scan in six months. I was elated to hear the miraculous news of God's blessing.

Now as I was serving and networking in ministry, another ministry leader asked me to put my testimony on her blog, and so I agreed, and then she also posted it on Facebook and tagged me. After J saw this, she unfriended me on FB, and we had no further communication. I was extremely grieved over this last bit of connection being cut off, but I knew it was God's will, so I stayed on the course and worked through it with Him by my side.

The Christmas Fast and a Special Delivery

In December 2016, I was supposed to go to my brother's for Christmas in Florida. However, I got really sick with the flu and had to cancel my flight and stay home. I felt the Holy Spirit prompting me to fast for three days while I was sick and pray for J, so I did, starting on Christmas Eve and ending the day after Christmas. Then on Christmas Eve, I felt the Lord giving me a very distinct directive. He asked me to take the musical stuffed animal that looked like an angelic white horse that J gave me as a present one year and go buy a necklace with the word *love* on it and wrap it up in a box and bring it to her house. He also brought to mind a Christmas card that I had been saving for a special occasion with the picture of a Maltese that looked identical to the dog that we both loved and adored when we lived together. So I went to Walmart and found the necklace and placed it around the beautiful white horse's neck, placed it in a box, and wrapped it up in beautiful Christmas paper and a bow. I opened the Christmas card and began to write as I felt the Holy Spirit direct every word. It was such a surreal endeavor that is very hard to bring to life in words. As I was driving to J's house with the package on Christmas Eve, my good friend, Dee called me, and I pulled over as we prayed for God to do a major work through this special delivery. After several days, I texted J to make sure she received the package and she said that her neighbor gave it to her as I put it on the wrong front porch. When I realized that I put the package on the wrong porch, I was taken back that I didn't remember J's house as I had been there multiple times to help her move. I remember being really sick that night and not being sure which house was hers. Anyway, I was glad she received it and would pray that God would use this stuffed animal in a miraculous way to show her His love and redemption.

Stricken by Grief, Mad at God, Then Flooded with Joy

On February 14, I felt really sad and cried all day as though I was mourning J's passing. Then the next day on the fifteenth, there was a FB post that J had passed. I was still extremely sad but then became very *angry* with God as I thought He promised to heal J. This is one of the first times in my entire journey that I experienced being mad at God. I also know that we are human and experience human emptions. I trusted God and believed with all my heart that He was going to heal J. So I was mad and confused. I texted two ministry leaders to ask them to take my testimony off their websites as it was a *lie*. One of the leaders called me immediately after my text to pray with me, and as he was praying, he said, "I believe the Lord just gave me a word that she couldn't be more healed than being in her perfect, heavenly spirit in paradise." As he was speaking this word, a text came in from the other ministry leader confirming that exact statement. I was then immediately filled with the love of the Father as my heart was filled with overflowing joy. I may never know on this side of heaven what happened to her that night when she passed, but I believe with all my heart it was a supernatural event where God used that stuffed animal to pour out His love on her. Why would He ask me to fast for her and be so specific on what I was to deliver to her house? I believe my ultimate reward will be opening my eyes on that first vision of heaven and being greeted by Jesus with J at His side. What a day that will be! Hallelujah! Praise His name!

Moving Forward in His Call

God is faithful. I know this by personal experience and the trustworthiness of His Word. I continue to grow in my church and serve in ministry. God is calling me to be a *voice of His truth* in a society of deception. What a privilege to have this calling and to be engaged with so many others like myself that God has redeemed in this way. I'm so glad I heeded his "wake-up call." This new life is not without its challenges. I'm still working through so much, but He is right there with me daily, making Himself more and more known to me. I wouldn't trade this new life for anything. I feel more alive than ever!

One major verse the Lord gave me as I continue to go through the process of healing is about the power of the testimony.

They triumphed over him by the blood of the Lamb and by the word of their testimony; they did not love their lives so much as to shrink from death. (Revelation 12:11)

They *triumphed* ("overcame, victory, conquered") by the blood of the Lamb and the word of their testimony. By "the blood of the Lamb" is the ground or reason for our victory. There is no victory without the sacrifice. We are so unclean by our sin and therefore unable to have a connection with God. But through the precious blood of Jesus Christ, we can be cleansed from all our sins and unrighteousness if we believe and confess. This allows us access to our Creator. Not only access but access to the power of God in our lives: the power of the resurrection. *Wow*, we should be shouting this from the rooftops!

How do others find out about this redeeming love? By the word of our testimony. When we keep things in the dark, Satan can use it to keep us in bondage with shame and guilt. It is only when we bring those things into the light that God can release us from this bondage. Only Jesus can transform our hearts, but we must be ready and willing to accept truth and obey God's Word. We must humble ourselves before God and ask Him to reveal anything in our lives that we haven't dealt with through repentance and prayer. God already knows our secrets and is waiting for us to release them and seek His process of healing. Sometimes we can deal with it on our own with the Holy Spirit's help, and sometimes we may need to share it with those in our close circle who can support and uplift us through the healing process. Then after we receive some form of healing, God may ask us to share it with others to help them feel safe to share their secrets to receive God's redeeming healing *power*.

When our hearts are right with Him, He will guide us to give our testimony at His appointed times and places. Our testimonies release God's transforming power into the prepared hearts to receive it. It is truly all God and for His glory. We just get to watch and obey and be in *awe* of how truly amazing and loving our God is about each one of us.

What does the end of that verse say? They did not love their lives so much as to shrink from death. Their value was not in themselves or what they did. It was in God and all for His honor and glory. Their testimonies would release His redeeming love and power into the prepared hearts and open minds to receive God's gift of salvation. God's love is so overpowering that it would bring them to a place of complete surrender. They would lay down their lives (physical death, the short side of eternity) for Him (love God) and His people (love people).

This Bible study is called *Living in Victory*, and we can only do that through Jesus Christ. He is our victory. We must give Him our all! Every part of us, not just the parts we are okay with giving Him but the parts that are very difficult. What are your difficult parts? Give them all to Him. Truly surrender all.

> Search me, O God, and know my heart;
> Try me, and know my anxieties;
> And see if there is any wicked way in me,
> And lead me in the way everlasting. (Psalm 139:23–24)

Where are you in your walk with God? Let's pray right now that God will be with us today and show us during this study where we are according to God's plan for our lives and that we will do whatever He asks us to do in order to walk on His glorious path of victory.

BIBLE STUDY TOOLS
AND DEFINITIONS

Definitions

A *cross-reference* is another verse in the Bible that has a similar theme or topic as the verse you are reading. Many of the Bible study apps below will have them listed as you select specific verses.

Commentary can usually be found in a study Bible at the bottom of the page with the verse(s) listed in bold. Then you will find a written explanation and interpretation of those verses. You can also find great commentary in the study apps listed below.

These tools will really help you dive deep in this study and this is where God meets us in the study and mediating of His Word. If you are unfamiliar with the Bible Study tools below, just Google them and type in training and see if you can find a training video.

Bible Study Applications

My favorite online Bible resource tools
http://BlueLetterBible.org (Diving deeper into the Greek and Hebrew)
https://www.olivetree.com (This is my favorite Bible study app for my computer and phone.)
https://www.youversion.com/ (Bible Study App and Social Media Community)
http://Biblehub.com (Easy Bible Study Website and App)

Discussion and Study Guide

This Bible study is all about victory in Christ. Before we can begin on the path of victory to know God's will, we must clear the path. Before God can work in us, we must have a pure heart.

Blessed are the pure in heart, for they will see God. (Matthew 5:8)

Who shall ascend into the hill of the Lord? or who shall stand in his holy place? He that hath clean hands, and a pure heart; who hath not lifted up his soul unto vanity, nor sworn deceitfully. (Psalm 24:3–4)

How do we obtain a pure heart? Submitting ourselves unto God and seeking Him with a humble heart to reveal any unconfessed sin—acknowledging that sin, confessing it, and turning from it.

Another area that clears the path is submitting our will, pride, strong desires, and dreams, and saying to God, "Not my will but Your will be done." You may say, "there is too much in my life, and I'm not ready to deal with all of this." I know *I* have a lot to deal with too. That is okay—we all do! God just asks us for a willing heart to get started. The enemy will tell you this is too hard, you can't possibly do all of this. You will have to give up this or that. Don't listen to his lies. God just wants us to start with getting close to Him and seeking His face, and He will guide you step by step. This study will help you take each step in God's timing. You may not get it all in seven weeks, but that is okay. Just start and seek God, and He will take you by the hand and lead you in His gentle, loving way. Just like a loving Father leads His children, first we crawl, then we walk and stumble, then we walk firmly. My goal for you during this study is that you will find out where you stand in your walk with God and have a clear direction and understanding on the roads to take on your victory journey with God.

Your appointment with God is?_____set your alarm and fill in your calendar! He is the VIP in your life on this short side of eternity and for *all eternity*!

Memory Verse

Search me, O God, and know my heart;
Try me, and know my anxieties;
And see if there is any wicked way in me,
And lead me in the way everlasting. (Psalm 139:23–24)

Please write this verse on a card, or put it in the notes section in your phone, or better yet, put it as a morning alert on your phone for each day of this week. Not only memorize it but also pray it out loud to God every day and listen for His sweet, tender voice.

Make Him a priority, seek His face, and allow Him complete access to your heart. He will show you what is in your life that must be confessed or removed so that He can work. We all have something. If you are having difficulty coming up with anything, ask God if pride is something you need to deal with first. Pride is one of the most stubborn barriers to surrender. And one way to know for sure that you are dealing with pride is the thought that you don't have it.

The following sections are "Prayer" and "Questions." Try to pray this prayer every day, and review the questions. Don't be in a rush to get them answered. Seek the Lord for the answers, and watch how He directs you to certain ones during your daily reading and meditation with Him.

Prayer

Lord, show me anything that is hindering my walk with You. Is there any sin in my life that I am not aware of or that I am aware of but don't want to give up? Is there someone I need to forgive? Are there any personal or family secrets that I am afraid to face? Do I put my plans as priority without seeking You first?

Show me, Lord, if I am putting anything before You. Is it a person? Is it a dream? Is it a position? Is it wealth? Is it popularity? Is it my time? Is it *pride*?

Now be quiet before the Lord, and wait on Him to answer you. Get some paper, and start writing what He reveals to you. This is the most important step in this entire study! Please don't move forward in this study until your heart is ready to surrender and hear what He has to say. If you don't hear anything, then put the study down and try again later. Maybe sit before the Lord, and read scripture and pray. Once you know what He is saying, then you will be led by the Holy Spirit to wholeness. Otherwise, you will be moving forward in the flesh, and the study will not be effective toward your spiritual wholeness.

Daily Reading

Meditate on the verses each day. Take some time to look up any cross-reference verses in the margin and read any commentary in your Bible or Bible study app.

Questions

What is God saying to you when you pray that prayer?

Can you hear Him? If not, why? Are you making time with Him without distractions? Does He have a slot in your schedule?

What is God showing you?

Where are you in your life's journey? Are you on your own path, *or* do you know for sure you are following God's plan?

Has God ever shown you something specific He wanted you to do? How did you respond?

How did you know it was from Him?

Write down some blessings that God has done in your life to share with a group or friend.

What is He doing now in your life? What are your challenges in hearing from God?

Day 1

Read Psalm 40:1–4: "I waited patiently and expectantly for the Lord…"

Write the verse here:

List a few cross-references here, and pick one that stands out, and mediate on it or share it with someone if you are doing this study with a group.

Did anything in the commentary stand out to you?

What did you hear?

What do you think?

What will you do?

What is your prayer?

Day 2

Read 2 Peter 1:3–11: "Make your calling sure…"

Write the verse here:

List a few cross-references here, and pick one that stands out to meditate on and/or share with someone.

Did anything in the commentary stand out to you?

What did you hear?

What do you think?

What will you do?

What is your prayer?

Day 3

Read Psalm 15:1–5: "Who may live on your holy hill?"

Write verse here:

List a few cross-references here, and pick one that stands out to meditate on and/or share with someone.

Did anything in the commentary stand out to you?

What did you hear?

What do you think?

What will you do?

What is your prayer?

Day 4

Read Proverbs 3:5–6: "Trust in the Lord…"

Write verse here:

List a few cross-references here, and pick one that stands out to meditate on and/or share with someone.

Did anything in the commentary stand out to you?

What did you hear?

What do you think?

What will you do?

What is your prayer?

Day 5

Read Romans 8:28: "And we know…"

Write verse here:

List a few cross-references here, and pick one that stands out to meditate on and/or share with someone.

Did anything in the commentary stand out to you?

What did you hear?

What do you think?

What will you do?

What is your prayer?

LIVING IN VICTORY

Day 6

Read Psalm 1:1–3: "Blessed is the one..."

Write verse here:

List a few cross-references here, and pick one that stands out to meditate on and/or share with someone.

Did anything in the commentary stand out to you?

What did you hear?

What do you think?

What will you do?

What is your prayer?

WEEK 2

Beginning the Journey Out of Death and Into Life

Last Week's Review

Before we can move forward on the journey, we must clear the path.

This week is going to start us on the journey with God. However, before we can move forward, the path must be clear. This was our task in week 1. If you didn't have a chance to do this yet, set aside some time with the Lord and seek Him with a humble heart, ready and willing to receive what He says. Pray this verse out loud and ask Him to reveal what you need to lay down at the foot of the cross:

Search me, O God, and know my heart;
Try me, and know my anxieties;
And see if there is any wicked way in me,
And lead me in the way everlasting. (Psalm 139:23–24)

Okay, so did you ask God to show you what you need to lay down at the foot of the cross? Did He show you? Are you resisting it? What is stopping you?

Has God asked you to lay something down that you treasure or do something that you hate? If you think it is impossible, it is without God's help, but we must have a willing spirit to lay it down no matter what the costs. We must surrender our pride and self-will, and when we do, watch and see the true plan of God come alive in your life. It may not be easy at first. There may be many obstacles, but keep your eyes on Jesus and just take one step at a time. God will bring you through each one and prepare you for the next. Every relationship has two parts, and our part is to obey and leave all the consequences to Him.

Getting to Know God by Seeking the Things Above

God gave me the wisdom to realize that the first half of my life with me as the driver was a disaster. *Now* I am so ready to hand Him the keys. It was very difficult for a control freak like me, but I knew His plan was better than the mess I had made. God was so gentle, and He taught me at a slow, steady pace to trust Him and to have patience. I was very fortunate as I was all alone. At first, it was scary, but He gave me comfort as time went on. In my quiet time with God, I would listen and hear what God was directing me to do next. It is crucial to have quite time with God. If you don't have a place, make a place. This is something that took me a while to get used to as I was always doing and going and making *my* activities priority over God. I am a driven person and didn't believe in wasting any time. But God showed me that this is the most precious time we can make away from all the busy, distracting noise of the world. Have you noticed that there is a TV screen or multiple TV screens almost in every public place you go?

Therefore, if you have been raised up with Christ, keep seeking the things above, where Christ is, seated at the right hand of God. Set your mind on the things above, not on the things that are on earth. (Colossians 3:1–2)

This verse has a special meaning to me as it has opened my spiritual eyes. When I watch people, we are all so *busy*, moving at a hundred miles an hour. I heard one preacher say that "BUSY" stands for "Burdened Under Satan's Yoke." I believe that is a great depiction of the word.

What are we all so busy doing? Do these activities bring us closer to God or our worldly pleasures and accolades, which will all fade away on this short side of eternity? God showed me that making Him priority is what I had to do to experience the fullness of His presence. He gave me a desire to read His Word and make His Word the priority of my schedule by starting each day reading, meditating, and studying it. He would show me all kinds of wonderful pleasures in His Word and give me the peace, joy, and strength I needed for the day. He would then allow my day to flow in harmony as everything would just fall into place. The stress of the day would subside with God's presence of peace, knowing that He is now in control of my life, my day, and every little circumstance that would come my way. I can now understand and experience the true meaning of this verse.

And the peace of God, which passeth all understanding, shall keep your hearts and minds through Christ Jesus. That peace that passes all understanding. (Philippians 4:7)

So Why Is the Bible So Important in This Process of Getting to Know God?

For the word of God is alive and active. Sharper than any double-edged sword, it penetrates even to dividing soul and spirit, joints and marrow; it judges the thoughts and attitudes of the heart. (Hebrews 4:12)

The Bible is not any ordinary book! It is *alive* and *active*! What does that mean? Just looking up the word *alive* in Strong's Concordance, here are a few words that describe *alive*: "living water, having vital power in itself, and exerting the same upon the soul; to be fresh, strong, efficient."

The Word became flesh and made his dwelling among us. We have seen his glory, the glory of the one and only Son, who came from the Father, full of grace and truth. (John 1:14)

The "Word" is Jesus, who came to earth to dwell among us.

So here is a book that is alive and active and is Jesus? But why don't we read it? Why isn't it a priority? I *know* why! The enemy is the ruler of this world, and if he can keep you from this book, his job becomes easy as you fall into the messages and doldrums of this world.

In which you used to live when you followed the ways of this world and of the ruler of the kingdom of the air, the spirit who is now at work in those who are disobedient. (Ephesians 2:2)

The enemy will do everything he can to keep you from picking up this book. I can guarantee that when a believer determines to make God and His Word a priority, they will experience an immediate distraction the moment they pick it up. I have had many friends tell me that is exactly what happens to them but knowing this ahead of time really helped them become proactive to eliminate most known distractions and increases awareness to ignore any that may arise. There is now even a screen we carry around with us that brings so many distractions. We must be very intentional to keep the distractions out so we can sit with God in His Word. I know this is a major struggle that we all deal with so I ask that we all pray for each other in this area to make a place free of distractions to seek our Lord and find out what He is saying for today.

You are in a meeting with the King of kings and Lord of lords! *Nothing* should be allowed to interrupt this time with God.

Hearing from God

Once we make Him a priority and read His Word, then we need to be sensitive to hearing His voice. Is this an audible voice? For some, it could be. I have never heard the Lord audibly. For me, it starts in the heart and is translated in the mind. So as I continued to seek God in my morning devotions during my process to wholeness, I would always pray for Him to reveal His will for that day and for my life. I was ready to go! I wanted to serve my risen Savior who pulled me out of the pit of death. But I didn't hear anything except one thing over and over. I kept hearing, *Get to know Me first. Wait on* Me. I would hear *wait* everywhere I turned, every devotional and sermon I listened to. So I waited! God also revealed that I needed to spend time with Him so I can grow closer to Him, which provides the strength and power of the Holy Spirit to avoid the *pit*-falls of Satan. This takes time, as He puts us through training. A solder has to go through serious training before they can be sent into battle and experience victory. So we wait and spend time with God as He continues to mold and train us for His victory plan. He will reveal His plan one strategy at a time. He will test us to see if we follow His direction or divert to the path of our own desires. Will we be lured onto the path with more popularity, action, and excitement; or will we be content in the quietness with God?

What Is Our Priority?

Where is your focus these days? Our society is so focused on sports, and that is fine in balance. However, where does family devotion time, prayer time, and Christian community fall on our priority list? One area that is a challenge for me is technology. We forget our cell phones, and we have to go back to get them. We have to make sure not to miss a text or FB message and see how many likes we have. What about prayer? Do we make sure not to forget to talk with God? Instead of lunch plans, do we set up prayer plans with our friends? How much time do we spend worshiping and serving God? These are the activities that should be first on our list as these activities further the kingdom of God and are the only activities that have an everlasting value.

So whether you eat or drink or whatever you do,
do it all for the glory of God. (1 Corinthians 10:31)

Do we really believe this verse? Then why don't we follow it? Because it is impossible in our human state—flesh. We must be "plugged into the Power Source" in order to obtain it. That means making God a *priority* in our life.

Trusting God with All Our Heart

Trust in the Lord with all your heart,
And lean not on your own understanding;
In all your ways acknowledge Him,
And He shall direct your paths. (Proverbs 3:5–6)

God's Will, Not Our Will

I believe one of the key factors to finding God's will for our lives is complete surrender of our will and pride. Letting go of our pride and self-will is one of the most difficult tasks and strongest traits of our human nature (the flesh) to break. It was the main cause for the fall of mankind when Eve was tempted in the garden to disobey God's instruction and follow her own desires. To die to self is a constant battle and can't be fought alone. We will only have success if we seek God in prayer and do our part to obey His Word. We must also put on the full armor of God and surround ourselves with prayer warriors who will support us during the difficult times. As we continue to die to self and the flesh, He will continue to renew us each day with His life-giving Sprit. The Spirit will help us each step of the way as long as we continue to move forward on God's path. We will continue to grow and take on the traits of Jesus, and only through Him can we truly experience God's transforming power.

What does this mean in the practical sense? It could mean that we may have to encourage someone else to do what we thought we were supposed to do. It may mean giving of ourselves without any recognition at all. It may mean being under someone's authority that treats us unfairly. It may mean forgiving someone who hurt us deeply. When we surrender our will and pride, this allows God full reign in our hearts to release His transforming power in our lives.

So how did God show me to lay down my will for His will? First, I had to determine that I was going to do whatever He told me to do even if I didn't like it, even if I hated it. During my morning appointments with God, I would ask Him to show me His will and then listen for His voice. This usually happens when we are in His Word.

As I continued to spend time getting to know God and waiting for direction, I will never forget His first request. When you first hear God, it's hard to determine if this is Him or your own thoughts, but He will tell you over and over. As you grow closer to God, He doesn't have to repeat Himself over and over unless you refuse to listen. So here I was, getting my first directive from God. Do you think I was excited? *No way!* I couldn't believe what I was hearing. He wanted me to go back into nursing and renew my license that I had let expire after ten years. At the time, my passion and drive was working my Internet marketing and design company. However, I was determined to follow God and His will no matter what. I knew my plans didn't work. So I kept hearing the word nursing everywhere. I didn't like nursing. I had to follow procedures, stay within guidelines, and adhere to rigid regulations. This was torture to my creative mind. However, I kept hearing *nursing*, so I decided to be obedient even though the thought of nursing was very stressful to me. So I had two choices: I could either go to school and participate in clinical for three months or study and retake the boards. So I decided to study and take the boards. I purchased the study books and studied day and night for three months. I finally took the boards. During the test, I recall all the questions seemed completely foreign to my studies. I couldn't believe how the questions were worded. I paid a fee to get my results early. Two weeks after the test, I went online to check the status, and it stated that my results would be ready in a few minutes, so I waited.

As soon as the results were ready, I clicked on the link, and the word *failed* was revealed. I was instantly disappointed. I had never failed anything in my life. However, as soon as the word *failed* was revealed online, in came an e-mail from my church with the subject line "Social Media for Brookwood." I felt God say to my heart, *You obeyed Me and passed My test, and now I am giving you the desires of your heart. You will now use your marketing business for My kingdom to fulfill the Great Commission online where millions can be reached around the world.* Wow, what a moment. God had given me instant joy from a moment of failure. I had previously met with Brookwood folks to see if they could use my services, and now their response came in God's perfect timing. However, God wanted me to take my commitment even further and deliver my services for free as a tithe. I would obey whatever God told me to do as I knew in my heart He had the best plan for me. I also knew that His promises and blessings wouldn't come without a sacrifice on my part. I kept thinking back to Abraham and everything God asked him to do before he could receive his promise of blessings.

Discussion and Study Guide

Your appointment with God is—set your alarm and fill in your calendar! He is the VIP in your life on this short side of eternity and for *all eternity*!

Memory Verse

Trust in the Lord with all your heart,
And lean not on your own understanding;
In all your ways acknowledge Him,
And He shall direct your paths. (Proverbs 3:5–6)

Please write this verse on a card, and put it in the notes or reminders section in your phone. Not only memorize it but also say it out loud.

Discussion Questions

What does your schedule look like?

Who or what gets priority in your schedule? What drives this priority?

When you need to make a decision, do you seek God and wait for the answer? Why or why not?

Who is in the driver's seat of your life? Who do you think has the best GPS route for your life? Do these two match?

Have you ever asked God if there is anything in your schedule that He wants you to remove? What is it?

How often do you read God's Word, the Bible? Is this a chore, or do you take delight in it as you would your favorite activity? If it is a chore, why do you think that is the case?

Share some blessings that God has done in your life this week.

Share some insights into what God is showing you through this study.

Prayer

Lord, help me to put You first in my life. Help me to know what it means to delight in Your Word. I pray that You will remind me and help me to spend time in Your Word every day. Help me to seek You on all decisions. Help me be patient and wait for Your answer before moving forward in my own strength.

Daily Reading

Meditate on the verses each day. Take some time to look up any cross-reference verses in the margin and read any commentary in your Bible or Bible study app.

Day 1

Read Colossians 3:1–17.

List a few cross-references here, and pick one that stands out to meditate on and/or share with someone.

Did anything in the commentary stand out to you?

What did you hear?

What do you think?

What will you do?

What is your prayer?

Day 2

Read Matthew 6:33: "Seek ye first the Kingdom of God…"

Write the verse here:

List a few cross-references here, and pick one that stands out to meditate on and/or share with someone.

Did anything in the commentary stand out to you?

What did you hear?

What do you think?

What will you do?

What is your prayer?

Day 3

Read Psalm 127:1: "Unless the Lord builds the house…"

Write verse here:

List a few cross-references here, and pick one that stands out to meditate on and/or share with someone.

Did anything in the commentary stand out to you?

What did you hear?

What do you think?

What will you do?

What is your prayer?

Day 4

Read Psalm 119.

You don't have to write the verses today. But do take your time with this chapter as it provides nourishment to the soul that will keep you refreshed throughout the day.

Did anything in the verses or commentary stand out to you?

What did you hear?

What do you think?

What will you do?

What is your prayer?

Day 5

Read Matthew 6:19–21: "For where your treasure is…"

Write verse here:

List a few cross-references here, and pick one that stands out to meditate on and/or share with someone.

Did anything in the commentary stand out to you?

What did you hear?

What do you think?

What will you do?

What is your prayer?

Day 6

Read 1 Corinthians 10:31: "Do *all* for the Glory of God…"

Write verse here:

List a few cross-references here, and pick one that stands out to meditate on and/or share with someone.

Did anything in the commentary stand out to you?

What did you hear?

What do you think?

What will you do?

What is your prayer?

Sowing to the Spirit and Starving the Flesh

The choice of a victorious life is all ours. God gave us a freewill to choose life or death. We can have victory or live a defeated Christian life. We can continually struggle, or we can have abundance in Christ.

> Don't you know that when you offer yourselves to someone as obedient slaves, you are slaves of the one you obey—whether you are slaves to sin, which leads to death or slaves to obedience, which leads to righteousness? (Romans 6:15–16, NKJV)

Once we are in complete obedience to God, then and only then can He start working in our lives.

As I continued to seek God for direction, He gave me a very specific task to do. He wanted me to starve the flesh and feed my Sprit. He also gave me the wisdom through His Word on how to do it.

> Be not deceived; God is not mocked: for whatso-
> ever a man soweth, that shall he also reap. For he that
> soweth to his flesh shall of the flesh reap corruption;
> but he that soweth to the Spirit shall of the Spirit reap
> life everlasting. (Galatians 6:7–8)

He had me analyze everything that I allowed into my life and determine which areas were feeding the flesh and which areas were feeding the Spirit.

He gave me the wisdom to understand at the very beginning of this process that if I closed all doors that were open to feeding the flesh (Satan's access points), He could really work in my life to transform it and bring the blessings that He promised.

So what is the flesh? The flesh is a combination of the physical body and the soul (mind, will, and emotions). The flesh is human nature apart from God.

The Spirit is the Holy Spirit that is planted inside of you when you are born again by accepting Christ into your life. You now have a new nature that will continue to grow more like Christ every day as long as you continue in His ways to feed and nurture your Spirit.

How can we measure if we are feeding the flesh or the Sprit?

Well, if we are feeding the Spirit, then we will bear the fruit of the Sprit. And if we are feeding the flesh, we will exhibit the destructive traits of the flesh.

Spirit	Flesh
Love	Hate,
Joy	Strife, anger, angry undercurrent
Peace	Fear
Contentment	Envy, jealousy
Goodness	Bitterness, unforgiveness
Faithfulness	Wavering
Patience	Worry, anxiety
Being mild-tempered	Being easily offended and mad, flying off the handle.
Kindness, selflessness, serving	Selfishness, self-centeredness, pride, self-promotion, usury

The Victory Formula

Blessed is the one who does not walk in step with the wicked or stand in the way that sinners take or sit in the company of mockers, but whose delight is in the law of the Lord, and who meditates on His Law day and night. That person is like a tree planted by streams of water, which yields its fruit in season and whose leaf does not wither—whatever they do prospers. (Psalm 1:1–3)

I love this verse! I believe that this verse provides the *truth* for victory in Christ! We don't have to struggle (not saying we won't struggle at times), but it takes delighting in the Law of the Lord—His Word, the Bible—being close to Him and *not* allowing the world's messages to influence us.

Do not sit in the company of mockers. Who are the mockers of Christ? Do you watch shows, movies, or listen to music that take our Lord's name in vain? How about shows that promote self-worship and leave God out of the picture? You are either living a self-centered life or a God-centered life. If you subject yourself to worldly Hollywood messages (yes, I said it, Hollywood—everything about it *stinks!*), then you can expect to struggle. Some movies may be G-rated, but you are supporting the entire industry that mocks Christians and our precious Lord and Savior, Jesus Christ. If you listen to the world's messages, you are opening a door for Satan's influences. Even if the message seems innocent, it is still the world's message and *not* God's—a message that feeds the flesh and not the Spirit, a message that says you know better than God, and you can do it all without Him. You become the superhero! But we are *nothing* without Christ! And yet we can do all things through Christ.

God warns us to guard our hearts actually He puts a high priority on it...

> Above all else, guard your heart, for everything you do flows from it. (Proverbs 4:23, NIV)

I know this may be a strong message, but Christians *today* are becoming more and more like the world and wondering why they constantly struggle. They are more worried about being relevant than having righteousness. We are *not* to blend in with the world. It is getting dark out there, and all the signs of the Lord's return are at hand. However, only God knows when, but He gives us signs; and believe me, those signs are growing exponentially. It's time to stand up! It is time to be the *salt* and *light!* I believe God has put a fire in me to help wake Christians up and start standing for the truth in God's Word. The United States of America is successful because the founding fathers were guided by the principles of God's Word.

What about social media? If you knew the Lord was coming back tomorrow, what would you post on Facebook? Aren't we supposed to live that way every day?

Some of the posts I see from Christians make my stomach turn. I see posts about celebrities, alcohol, and seductive pictures. Don't you know you could be subjecting someone who is weak in that area to fall? Your intention may be innocent, but have some discernment. What does the message say? Is the picture seductive in anyway? Why would a Christian post such trash? Talk about the Lord and tell your friends what He has done for you today.

So whether you eat or drink or whatever you do,
do it all for the glory of God. (1 Corinthians 10:31)

What do you think this verse is saying? Do you really believe it? Should you be living it?

We are in dark times. Christians are being silenced, and one day, we won't be able to talk about God *at all* on social media without a fine or being shut down. Many conservative voices have already been shut down on social media. We are approaching a very critical time when Christians in the USA who stand for truth (God's Word) and righteousness will be persecuted even by their own fellow believers. The Word says that before Jesus returns there will be a great falling away which we are seeing now. So the choice we all need to make is…will we stand for truth and righteousness no matter the cost or will we fall by the wayside into the ways of this world? I will say this…those who are in the Word seeking God's will for their life will have a much better chance of standing firm and following God's path.

But small is the gate and narrow the road that leads
to life and only a few find it. (Matthew 7:14, NIV)

Do not conform to the pattern of this world but be transformed by the renewing of your mind. Then

you will be able to test and approve what God's will is—
his good, pleasing and perfect will. (Romans 12:2 NIV)

We must *know* our enemy, or there is no victory to be won.
He certainly knows all about us. He studies us and knows our
weaknesses and when to attack. When Satan tempted Jesus in
the wilderness, he said, "Bow down to me" (just once). Go just
a little below what you know is right. If Jesus had done this, we
wouldn't be here today.

No wonder, for even Satan disguises himself as
an angel of light. (1 Corinthians 11:14 NASB)

We like the things of this world: secular music and TV
shows. Okay, so you screen those and don't allow too many curse
words. What about God's name being taken in vain? Do you
turn off the show after you hear it once? Or do you have to
hear it three times? What about the shows with no language
or sex? What messages do they send out? Be all you can be: the
best. God's Word says we are nothing without Him. What about
the song "Happy," which is an innocent song and makes us feel
good? What is the message? Happy is the truth! Really, the truth
is connected to our feelings? No way! There is only one *truth*,
and it isn't connected to our feelings at all. You may think this
is so innocent, and that I am being totally legalistic. However,
words have *power*, and what we allow into our brains influence our thoughts, and thoughts can become actions. Happy
is the truth? As long as I am happy, I have truth? You are being
deceived but in a happy way. In the last days, it will be really
hard to discern the truth unless we are in God's Word and sensitive to the Holy Spirit's leading. The deception will be so great
and even use scripture to back up its messages. So it is crucial for
us to read the Word, delight in the Word, study the Word, and

mediate on the Word because we *love* it. Remember, the Word became flesh, and if you really love Jesus, you'll *love* His Word. The Love of God brings the Holy Spirit to guide us into all wisdom, truth, and discernment to keep us safe. It will be vital to stay in tune with the promptings of the Holy Spirit and to obey those promptings at onset to remain in Victory in these last days.

Discussion and Study Guide

Discussion Questions and Exercise for This Week

What are you feeding? I challenge you to make a list of your daily activities and write them down. Check off the ones that feed the Spirit. Do these activities fall under your plan as items that feed the flesh, or do these items fall under God's plan as items that feed the Spirit?

We all have to live in this world and do human-nature tasks to keep this flesh suit alive. However, we need to make God and His will our priority in order to fulfill and live in the abundance of His plan for our lives. This is a process and won't happen overnight. Look at your list. Pick a few areas that feed the flesh, and substitute those areas with things that feed the Spirit. For example, say you listen to secular music 80 percent of the time and Christian music 20 percent of the time. Increase that percentage as God directs you to. For me, God wanted me to immediately remove secular music and replace it with Christian music.

Look at the shows you watch on TV. Ask yourself, what is the central message of the show? Is that message in line with God's truths? Replace those shows with Christian TV, CDs, DVDs, and Christian blogs and books. Watch a Christian movie or series on TBN. *Travel the Road* is an awesome series about two young guys who love the Lord, who go to the remote places of the earth to reach the untouchables, and it will totally warm your heart as you watch the natives respond to God's truth. The production is very similar to a survivor-type show. We are so blessed in America to have such an array of Christian media choices.

What gets priority on your calendar?

How is family time spent? Vacations and sports versus prayer and Bible study?

Whom do you write checks to?

What organizations do you support?

Prayer

Lord, show me the areas in my life where I am feeding my flesh that allow Satan access (open doors) into my thoughts and emotions. Show me how I might shut those doors, and substitute activities that feed my spirit so that I might grow in the grace and knowledge of my Lord and Savior, Jesus Christ.

Daily Reading

Meditate on the verses each day. Take some time to look up any cross-reference verses in the margin, and read any commentary in your Bible or Bible study app.

Day 1

Read Galatians 5:13–26.

List a few cross-references here, and pick one that stands out to meditate on and/or share with someone.

Did anything in the commentary stand out to you?

What did you hear?

What do you think?

What will you do?

What is your prayer?

Day 2

Read Galatians 6:1–10.

List a few cross-references here, and pick one that stands out to meditate on and/or share with someone.

Did anything in the commentary stand out to you?

What did you hear?

What do you think?

What will you do?

What is your prayer?

Day 3

Read Psalm 127:1.

Write verse here:

List a few cross-references here, and pick one that stands out to meditate on and/or share with someone.

Did anything in the commentary stand out to you?

What did you hear?

What do you think?

What will you do?

What is your prayer?

Day 4

Read Isaiah 55:6–11.

List a few cross-references here, and pick one that stands out to meditate on and/or share with someone.

Did anything in the commentary stand out to you?

What did you hear?

What do you think?

What will you do?

What is your prayer?

Day 5

Read Philippians 4:8–9.

Write verses here:

List a few cross-references here, and pick one that stands out to meditate on and/or share with someone.

Did anything in the commentary stand out to you?

What did you hear?

What do you think?

What will you do?

What is your prayer?

WEEK 4

Preparing for Battle

For our struggle is not against flesh and blood, but against the rulers, against the authorities, against the powers of this dark world and against the spiritual forces of evil in the heavenly realms. (Romans 6:15–16, NKJV)

We are in a *war* in the supernatural realm. This is really hard to grasp in the natural. Our society is filled with so many distractions to keep our focus on the "things of this earth" rather than the "things above." The more we intentionally focus on the things above, the more we realize and recognize the enemy's schemes.

The enemy is very clever, knows our strengths and weaknesses, and will take his time to carry out his plan. However, if we know this ahead of time and can learn to recognize his tactics, we can become proactive to thwart his fiery darts. I like to call this the "preen treatment." Preen is a weed preventer that stops weeds before they can take root. So once we learn to discern those negative thoughts and lies from the enemy, we need to take immediate action by taking those thoughts captive, praying with our close friends, and reading God's Word. You might ask, what does it mean to take my thoughts captive?

We demolish arguments and every pretension that sets itself up against the knowledge of God, and we take captive every thought to make it obedient to Christ. (2 Corinthians 10:5 NIV)

In this verse, "we demolish arguments and every pretension that sets itself up against the *knowledge of God.*" So in order to demolish, we must have the knowledge of God in our hearts and minds. How do we get this? By reading and meditating on His Word! You may be thinking, this seems to be a recurring theme in this Bible study. If you only get one thing from this study, this would be the *key takeaway* that I want you to get in order to have victory in Christ.

"And we take captive every thought to make it obedient to Christ." At first, I didn't really understand what taking my thoughts captive meant until I started watching Joyce Meyer. I knew that believers had the mind of Christ and can do all things through Him, but I didn't believe and understand it enough to apply it to my life.

When you decide to follow Christ and His plan, this wakes up the devil, and he starts to go to work. The enemy attacked my thoughts right from the start. When I decided to turn from my old life and follow God into the new life, I lost all my friends. I was very lonely, and this was not a surprise to Satan as he tried to use this to instill many negative thoughts to keep me down and depressed. However, I started attending church activities and meeting new friends. I was on fire for God and very excited about meeting new godly Christian women. I started serving at church in media production and started attending the WOW

(Women of the Word) Bible study every Wednesday. My loneliness started to subside as I continued to fellowship and serve with other believers.

However, I had a secret, and that secret caused me so much shame and guilt that I kept it to myself and let it fester inside. I thought, *What would they think of me? How would they respond?* These were all thoughts from the enemy to keep me in bondage, to keep me enslaved to fear. If he can keep us from opening up with others, he can keep us from the healing prayers and fellowship that come from our mature Christian brothers and sisters.

> Therefore, confess your sins to each other and pray for each other so that you may be healed. The prayer of a righteous person is powerful and effective. (James 5:15)

Buried secrets eat us alive. It wasn't until I opened up with my small group that I started to experience a true taste of freedom. I will never forget that day. I had been attending and serving in the church for over a year. I was actually back in the closet, but this time, it was the church closet. I had been waiting for the Lord to provide the opportunity for me to share my story. I had only shared my story with a few godly women with whom I felt safe and whom I could trust. I was testing the waters. The more I opened up and shared, the more freedom I felt from the shame and guilt—the more my heart could experience the true joy in Christ that would fill in those gaps.

Coming Out of the Church Closet

Today, June 19, was a day I could see God working all around me in a major way. It all started with a meeting at Brookwood with Tina at 9:00 a.m. We met about Brookwood social media, and she gave me a gift card for my help. The gift card had the following statement: "So let us never stop offering to God our praise through Jesus."

At about 9:55 a.m., a girl walked up to us to ask where she could find room E279, and I said she could follow me as I was headed to that room for a Beth Moore Bible study. Her name was Britt, and this was her first day to the church. It was as if God had directed her right to us. During the Bible study, my phone kept vibrating. It was a ministry leader, from a ministry in Spartanburg, that God would use to help me navigate the healing process and bring support during difficult times. This ministry helps those who want to find freedom from homosexuality in Jesus Christ. At first, I didn't answer since we were in the middle of the Bible study video. However, it kept vibrating over and over again as if it was an emergency, so I stepped out to take the call. He was so excited and had to share something that God put on his heart to encourage me. He was out running, and a girl ran past him, and she reminded him of me and then instantly he had this need to call to me, "A total God thing." So we talked for a short while as he was fired up with such an encouraging message of staying the course and running the race with God. I thanked him for the encouragement and went back to the Bible study.

During the sharing time in the Bible study, one new lady to our study named Tracy started talking about lesbians in her life. This started raising questions in the room, and one girl wanted to know how she should interact with them. I instantly locked eyes with Jill (one of my close friends whom I felt safe to share my story early on) knowing this was my cue to give my testimony. It was amazing how God gave me the words, and it totally touched the group, which opened the door for others to share secret struggles that they had been bearing alone. There is true power in the word of our testimony, and we should all be sharing when God leads us to share. At the end of the meeting, Tracy had the handful of women lay hands on me to pray. It was the most powerful, Spirit-led prayer experience I have ever had. This gave me the encouragement and support to move forward on my call from God. I also realized that the ministry leaders timing in his call was so divinely orchestrated as an encouraging sign from God before giving my testimony for the first time to a group of believers. It is so cool that God knows our every move before we make it, and He has already prepared the way. We just have to take the steps and walk in His guiding light.

Little did I know that God had a unique experience waiting for me on the other side of sharing my story that day. It is somewhat of an insider's blessing to those who watch Joyce Meyer. If you know the Joyce Meyer shopping cart story, you will understand what happens next; but if you don't, go ahead and google "Joyce Meyer shopping cart message." I had some things to pick up at Sam's Club and as I was looking for a place to park, I noticed not one shopping cart but two displaced in the parking lot so I decided to park next to them. One was the huge flat pallet type cart for hauling very large items and the other was a regular cart. Still basking in the blessings of the day, I decided I wanted more and determined to follow the practical teaching of Joyce in her shopping cart message. So I took the small cart to the cart area in the parking lot and hauled the big one into the store with me! I am so thankful that God used Joyce in teaching me so many truths in this season of my life! You may be thinking how can returning shopping carts be a blessing? Well, the best one to answer that question is Joyce. You will get a blessing if you watch her shopping cart message. What a day of overflowing *joy*. A day the Lord directs is far better than anything we can ever plan. Praise His holy name!

So now I was not only experiencing freedom in Christ, but I was also experiencing an increase in strength and courage from my sisters in Christ. What else do you think I was experiencing? If you guessed more attacks, you got it right. Not only the number of attracts grew but also the severity of the attacks. I felt a very strong oppression coming on. It was a dark oppression, and I knew it was from the enemy. I learned quickly to get with a core group of sisters to pray as this would lift some of the heaviness of the oppression. One saying from Joyce rang so true during this time: "New level, new devil." At times, I couldn't even get out of bed.

I started taking mild antidepressants. I had a really hard time taking these meds as I didn't want to rely on them instead of God. I prayed that if the Lord didn't want me to take them, my new doctor would discourage me from taking them. But that wasn't the case. She encouraged me to take them and said there wasn't anything wrong with it. So I kept taking them for a while, and they definitely helped me get out of bed and be productive during this difficult time. God gave me peace about this for a time but later started to convict me that I needed to rely on Him and not the meds. It took me a while to pass this test. There were days that I really struggled and just took the meds and asked God's forgiveness. Then there were days that I didn't take the meds and prayed for the Lord's strength to get through the day.

Over the course of time, the Lord would show me that the days I relied on Him were the days of abundant fruit-bearing activities; and the days I took the meds were the days that seem to go around in circles without any fruit-bearing activities whatsoever. I finally gave in and threw the meds in the toilet, and He helped me day by day to stay off them and showed me that I could get way more accomplished by relying on Him alone. Also, He started showing me healthy ways to increase my energy levels such as a healthy diet and exercise. We are so lazy as Americans; we want all the benefits of a healthy mind and body, but we don't want to do the work to get them.

Okay, here is a hard truth as I have said before! I believe God is calling me to help Christians wake up to the devil's lies, and this is one that I believe the enemy has duped many Christians. I believe Satan has *most* women who take antidepressants deceived into believing that they need them. When I took these drugs, they masked my true feelings and, I believe, hindered the presence of God in my life. Anything we do outside the will of God hinders His presence in our lives. I pray that if you are taking any meds, seek and ask God if He wants you to take them. You may have tried to come off them before and had a really bad experience. I know I did! I kept going back to them because I felt horrible without them. But remember, we can do *all things* through Christ, who strengthens us. Do we really believe that? God had to show me over and over again before I could let go of this *huge* stronghold that Satan had in my life. If this is something you struggle with, search in your area for a Celebrate Recovery program as this program is like AA but is centered on God's Word and the support of other believers.

More attacks were lobbed. I started having all kinds of negative thoughts about some of my friends, and this caused me to remain isolated and not have much trust in them. The enemy used the judgmental, critical, and suspicious mind that Joyce talks about in her book called *Battlefield of the Mind* to hinder my relationships. The Lord revealed to me that as a child, I grew up in a negative environment with the same suspicious mindset. As I prayed and sought God on how to deal with it, He gave me the wisdom to ignore those thoughts and pray for His truth to be revealed. The Holy Spirit taught me to pray and ask for God's blessings on those whom the bad feelings were directed. Eventually those feelings would subside where I could experience a new found peace and freedom in my soul.

The Armor of God

Finally, be strong in the Lord and in his mighty power. Put on the full armor of God, so that you can take your stand against the devil's schemes. For our struggle is not against flesh and blood, but against the rulers, against the authorities, against the powers of this dark world and against the spiritual forces of evil in the heavenly realms. Therefore, put on the full armor of God, so that when the day of evil comes, you may be able to stand your ground, and after you have done everything, to stand. Stand firm then, with the belt of truth buckled around your waist, with the breastplate of righteousness in place, and with your feet fitted with the readiness that comes from the gospel of peace. In addition to all this, take up the shield of faith, with which you can extinguish all the flaming arrows of the evil one. Take the helmet of salvation and the sword of the Spirit, which is the word of God. And pray in the Spirit on all occasions with all kinds of prayers and requests. With this in mind, be alert and always keep on praying for all the Lord's people. Pray also for me, that whenever I speak, words may be given me so that I will fearlessly make known the mystery of the gospel, for which I am an ambassador in chains. Pray that I may declare it fearlessly, as I should. (Ephesians 6:10–20 NIV)

The Bible teaches that Satan has waged war against God and His people. As in any battle, we must have the proper equipment to fight the enemy. However, this is a spiritual battle and not a physical one, so our weapons are not of this world. So let's get an understanding of what they are and how we can use them.

God provides all the battle gear we need but He requires us to activate them. The words *put on* mean that we have to take *action* on our end to have victory over the enemy.

1. **The belt of truth**. This is the first part of the armor because without truth, there is no source for victory. When we are rooted and grounded in the Word, we are a mighty strong tower immovable and ready to withstand any storm that may arise. When we commit ourselves daily to walk in God's truth, we are living in the safety of God's will. "Teach me your ways, O Lord, that I may live according to your truth!" (Psalm 86:11).

2. **The breastplate of righteousness**. A soldier wore this breastplate to protect the vital organs, the heart, and lungs. On the spiritual battlefield, it protects our heart from the wickedness of this world and all the deceptive emotions that lure us into sin.

3. **The gospel of peace**. Fitting our feet with the readiness that comes from the Gospel of peace. We can think of this as sturdy, protective footwear on the rocky

battlefield of the enemy, where we can stand firm with protection or move with quick agility to avoid the various traps that are set to slow us down from spreading the Gospel.

4. **The shield of faith** protects us from Satan's fiery darts, which are the lies that he implants in our minds. With the shield of faith, we can have confidence in God's trustworthiness and His unfailing faithfulness. This gives us the wisdom to cast down the lies of doubt and have confidence, knowing we are in the presence and power of the living God—the King of kings and Maker of heaven and earth.

5. **The sword of the Spirit** is God's Word, which can actually strike against Satan. "For the word of God is alive and active. Sharper than any double-edged sword, it penetrates even to dividing soul and spirit, joints and marrow; it judges the thoughts and attitudes of the heart" (Hebrews 4:12, NIV). When Jesus was tempted by the devil, He used Scripture to fight him, and he had to flee.

6. **The helmet of salvation** protects the head, where all thoughts and knowledge reside. "If you hold to my teaching, you are really my disciples. Then you will know the truth, and the truth will set you free" (John 8:31–32, NIV).

Discussion and Study Guide

Memory Verse

The Spirit of the Sovereign LORD is upon me,
for the LORD has anointed me
to bring good news to the poor.
He has sent me to comfort the brokenhearted
and to proclaim that captives will be released
and prisoners will be freed. (Isaiah 61:1)

So this verse says: He heals the brokenhearted, He opens prison doors, and He sets the captive free! Amen!

Discussion Questions and Exercise for This Week

What are your weaknesses? How do you think the enemy might attack you in this area?

Have you been able to analyze your thoughts and understand where they originate? From the world/enemy or from God/Bible?

It is vital to be in God's Word so you will have discernment to know God's truth, thereby being able to overcome the enemy's deception.

Name some thoughts from the enemy. We all have them, so don't be shy.

Name some thoughts from God's truth and His Word.

Who does God say you are?

Who does the world/enemy say you are?

Have you been able to take your thoughts captive? How?

How will you prepare for battle this week?

Prayer

Lord, let me come to you with a humble heart with no preconceived thoughts or ideas of my own. Lord, open my eyes to any area in which I am deceived and teach me Your truth. Let me see others and myself as You see us. Lord, help me understand my weaknesses and be proactive in this battle so that I may overcome enemy attacks at the onset. Lord, help me be diligent in my walk and to learn how to "put on" the full armor of God so that I may withstand the wiles of the devil and live in victory through Christ.

A Prayer from Scripture—Ephesians 3:14–21

For this reason, I kneel before the Father, from whom every family in heaven and on earth derives its name. I pray that out of his glorious riches He may strengthen you with power through his Spirit in your inner being, so that Christ may dwell in your hearts through faith. And I pray that you, being rooted and established in love, may have power, together with all the Lord's holy people, to grasp how wide and long and high and deep is the love of Christ, and to know this love that surpasses knowledge—that you may be filled to the measure of all the fullness of God.

Now to him who is able to do immeasurably more than all we ask or imagine, according to his power that is at work within us, to him be glory in the church and in Christ Jesus throughout all generations, for ever and ever! Amen.

Recommended Resource

Where is the devil's favorite place to attack? The mind! I highly recommend a book by Joyce Meyer called *Battlefield of the Mind: Winning the Battle in Your Mind.*

This book is an eye-opener and provides God's truth for victory in this area. Part 2 of her book discusses the conditions of the mind: a wandering, wondering mind; a confused mind; a doubtful and unbelieving mind; an anxious and worried mind; a judgmental, critical, and suspicious mind; a passive mind; and the mind of Christ.

Daily Readings

Meditate on the verses each day. Take some time to look up any cross-reference verses in the margin and read any commentary in your Bible.

Day 1

Read Ephesians 3:14–21.

The verses are printed on page 122 for you to pray each day as you seek the Lord.
List a few cross-references here, and pick one for us to read.

Did anything in the commentary stand out to you?

What did you hear?

What do you think?

What will you do?

What is your prayer?

Day 2

Read 2 Corinthians 10:1–6.

List a few cross-references here, and pick one for us to read.

Did anything in the commentary stand out to you?

What did you hear?

What do you think?

What will you do?

What is your prayer?

Day 3

Read Ephesians 6:10–20.

List a few cross-references here, and pick one for us to read.

Did anything in the commentary stand out to you?

What did you hear?

What do you think?

What will you do?

What is your prayer?

Day 4

Read Isaiah 61:1–3.

Please write this verse here.

List a few cross-references here, and pick one for us to read.

Did anything in the commentary stand out to you?

What did you hear?

What do you think?

What will you do?

What is your prayer?

Day 5

Read 2 Timothy 2:22–26.

List a few cross-references here, and pick one for us to read.

Did anything in the commentary stand out to you?

What did you hear?

What do you think?

What will you do?

What is your prayer?

_____

_____

_____

_____

_____

_____

_____

_____

_____

_____

_____

_____

_____

_____

_____

_____

_____

_____

_____

WEEK 5

Overcoming in the Battle

It is one thing to prepare for battle; it is another to get through it with victory. When we know our purpose in Christ and we begin to follow His lead, we must be prepared for intense spiritual warfare, and we must learn how to remain victorious through it. This is the ultimate trying of our faith but also the most rewarding.

> Consider it pure joy, my brothers and sisters, whenever you face trials of many kinds, because you know that the testing of your faith produces perseverance. Let perseverance finish its work so that you may be mature and complete, not lacking anything. If any of you lacks wisdom, you should ask God, who gives generously to all without finding fault, and it will be given to you. But when you ask, you must believe and not doubt, because the one who doubts is like a wave of the sea, blown and tossed by the wind. That person should not expect to receive anything from the Lord. Such a person is double-minded and unstable in all they do. (James 1:2–8)

Consider it pure joy when we face trials? How many of us can do this? In our human nature, it is extremely difficult; but in the supernatural, we can have success. We know that God "works everything for good to those who love Him and are called according to His purpose" (Romans 8:28). So if we love God and know we are following in His purpose, we can have the assurance that when we face trials, there is a purpose that is good—a perseverance that provides a mature spirit that is complete and lacks nothing. God give us wisdom but requires two actions on our part: to ask and to believe, and it will be given to us. But if we doubt, then we are double-minded and unstable in all we do.

Our feelings really keep us from having victory. We must ignore how we feel and *do* what we know is right even if we don't feel like it. Our feelings will usually catch up to our actions (if we persevere and do not faint). We must make a conscious effort to follow the Lord and obey His truth and let perseverance finish its work so that we can be complete and lack nothing. What a reward and promise for getting through our battles with the Lord.

God may have to take us around the same mountain over and over again until we understand and follow the path that He is directing. It may not be the path we had in mind. It may not look all that glamorous according to the world's standards, but it is the path of victory strategically laid out for you and me by God.

What are some of the obstacles that keep us going around the same mountain over and over again? Self-will and pride are the major destructive traits that keep us from climbing to the next level. We believe our intentions are good, but when we come before God with a surrendered heart and examine our motives in the light of Scripture, God will reveal our true intentions and help us align them with His truth. That is one area

God is showing me. I need to examine my true motives before I take action. For example, when I volunteer to serve or provide my services to a ministry or even post something on Facebook, I need to ask myself, what is driving me to do that? Is it for self-promotion, or is it to truly glorify God? If we determine our motives are self-serving, we can ask God for forgiveness and move on with pure intentions, which God can bless.

Paul realized that God gave him a thorn in the flesh to keep him humble.

> Even if I should choose to boast, I would not be a fool, because I would be speaking the truth. But I refrain, so no one will think more of me than is warranted by what I do or say, or because of these surpassingly great revelations. Therefore, in order to keep me from becoming conceited, I was given a thorn in my flesh, a messenger of Satan, to torment me. Three times I pleaded with the Lord to take it away from me. But he said to me, "My grace is sufficient for you, for my power is made perfect in weakness." Therefore, I will boast all the more gladly about my weaknesses, so that Christ's power may rest on me. That is why, for Christ's sake, I delight in weaknesses, in insults, in hardships, in persecutions, in difficulties. For when I am weak, then I am strong. (2 Corinthians 12:6–10)

God doesn't reveal the nature of Paul's thorn. This allows us to personalize Paul's experience to our own situation. What trial or trials are you experiencing right now? Is it an illness? Is it financial? Or is it a relationship? It is crucial that you give this burden to the Lord. Don't take it on yourself. Give it over to God. Get with Him every day in His Word. Seek Him and His presence, and you will gain strength to get through it. It is amazing how the pressure of that burden will get less and less as you give it to God (and keep giving it up). He may not remove it right away, and He may not remove it at all, but His strength is perfected in our weaknesses.

During a Bible study I attended on Gideon, God revealed this principle to me: His strength is perfected in our weaknesses. This revelation brought me to a whole new level of understanding the wisdom of God. You might be thinking--so I don't have to do all the work? *that's right,* Just ask for help and receive it! It is as simple as saying, "Jesus, help me, Jesus!" However, God may also want you to seek counsel or attend a support group that will build you up in the Lord and help keep you on track. Our spirit is willing, but our flesh is weak, so it is always good to have a group of godly Christians to keep us encouraged.

I love the way 2 Corinthians 12:9 is worded in the *Amplified Bible*:

> But He said to me, My grace (My favor and loving-kindness and mercy) is enough for you [sufficient against any danger and enables you to bear the trouble manfully]; for *My* strength *and* power are made perfect (fulfilled and completed) *and show themselves most effective* in [your] weakness. Therefore, I will all the more gladly glory in my weaknesses *and* infirmities, that the strength *and* power of Christ (the Messiah) may rest (yes, may pitch a tent over and dwell) upon me!

I just love the way God is leading this study. He is definitely working through me to write it. However, He is also having me attend His hands-on workshops so I can provide real-life experiences. I wasn't sure what to write about for this week, so I prayed for God to give it to me. I had to think back on each phase of how God worked with me to gain victory over my past. This week, He showed me that it is a continuous journey from glory to glory, that we will never fully "arrive" until we meet Him in glory. However, He will always be refining and sifting us to bring us closer and closer to His nature as we continue to delight in Him. If we are delighting in the world, we are constantly going to struggle in our walk with the Lord. We must determine in our hearts, enough is enough—die to self and seek God in *everything* we do.

So whether you eat or drink or whatever you do, do it all for the glory of God. (1 Corinthians 10:31 NIV)

Getting Through an Attack in Victory

So I thought I was set free from my same-sex attractions, but the enemy would once again pull the rug right out from underneath me at a ministry Conference in June of 2014. I just didn't see this coming, and it really shocked me and sent me on a roller coaster ride that would last for multiple years.

I was scheduled to give my testimony on Sunday and was very nervous about it being the first time at a major event. I was also warned by the executive director to be on my guard for major spiritual warfare. Well, I was hit hard with a strong attraction for one of the women participants at the conference. I thought, "What is this?" I thought I was healed from this struggle. I knew from the moment it started that I needed to bring it into the light, so I confessed it during my testimony that Sunday night and shared it with a close friend so we could pray. As I look back, I am very thankful for this experience as the Lord used it to sift and prune me by allowing the root issues to surface for major transformation, growth, and new experiences of walking in faith and repentance.

When we are going through a difficult time, it isn't fun when we're going through it, and many times, we will pray for God to remove it. However, we shouldn't do that but seek God on why we might be going through it. Is there a lesson or discipline He may want to reveal so that we can overcome that trial or struggle in the future and even use it to help others? When we can approach our trials with this perspective, we will experience what "Living in Victory" is all about. I once heard a saying that will keep this perspective fresh in your memory: "Try to find the treasure in the trial." It is probably from Joyce as I was saturated in her teachings daily!

Here are some key steps that fortified my process to healing in this area. First as soon as you experience bad thoughts, feelings, or temptations, take the thoughts captive through Christ. Sometimes, they just go away, but more times than not, they resurface. So for those that persist, bring them into the light immediately by confessing them to God and a trusted friend. Get on the phone or better yet in person so that you can pray with that person.

Second spend imitate time with the Lord, and journal as you study and mediate on the Word. Pray for God to bring you into community which is vital for long-term growth. Jesus had twelve disciples but only had three in His close circle. The close circle is where major healing can take place as you lay it *all* on the table; and everyone can speak to your blind spots and engage on a regular basis in close community for prayer, support, and accountability. The Holy Spirit taught me early on to bring my thoughts, feelings, and temptations into the light immediately. What does that look like to bring them into the light? It means to give the thoughts and desires to God immediately by taking the thoughts captive through Christ. If we keep our thoughts and feelings that we struggle with in the dark, we give the enemy access to torment us. He can't operate in the light. It also means staying in obedience to scripture and confessing and praying with a trusted friend. It may be different in each situation, so it is very important to seek God on how He wants you to bring it into the light. He may want you to confess the thoughts or feelings directly to the person you are having an issue with or not. You may need to ask forgiveness, especially if you have acted on any of those feelings. God knew I was going to face this trial, and so He prepared the way ahead of time and sent a soldier sister to come alongside me to be my support. This was totally not her type of conference, but she was obedient to God's call by completely stepping out of her comfort zone to be there for me at the conference. God is so good as He knows what we are going to face before we do. He knows our temptations, but He is faithful to be with us and provide godly counsel and support in our time of need.

I remember another time where my trial only lasted a weekend and where God removed it immediately. This attraction was to someone of the opposite sex (which I thought was good on one hand but not so good on the other as he was married). This attraction was one of the strongest I had ever experienced as it wouldn't leave me. Every thought was about this individual. I got in the Word. I prayed to take the thoughts captive. I rebuked the enemy, but the thoughts continued and just wouldn't leave. So I got on the phone and prayed with a close friend, and I thought that may have worked, but the thoughts came back and lasted all day. So I got on the phone with another friend, and that seemed somewhat better, but the thoughts came back, and they were tormenting. So I got on the phone again with a third friend who had the faith and took her authority in Christ that this would leave me, and after we prayed, the Lord covered me, and the thoughts left to never return. I believed the Lord used this experience to show me that if I am determined to remove my sinful thoughts and temptations, He is faithful and just to cleanse us from all unrighteousness.

> Be strong and courageous. Do not be afraid or terrified because of them, for the LORD your God goes with you; he will never leave you nor forsake you. (Deuteronomy 31:6)

A friend of mine, Tracy, said something very profound: "Satan usually works the hardest after a mountaintop experience."

Then it hit me—even though I was going through an attack, I did have a "mountaintop" experience at the Ministry Conference. Everyone who attended could not stop talking about how this conference was the best they had ever attended. The worship, the speakers, and the testimonies were all so uplifting and filled with the Spirit. The presence of God permeated the campus during the entire duration of the conference.

God also promises never to allow us to be tempted beyond what we can handle and will always provide for an escape.

> The temptations in your life are no different from what others experience. And God is faithful. He will not allow the temptation to be more than you can stand. When you are tempted, he will show you a way out so that you can endure. (1 Corinthians 10:13, NLT)

When the conference was over, I got home and crashed. What is it about "exercising" the spiritual nature and complete exhaustion (similar to a marathon in the natural)? I slept for almost two days straight with wakeful interludes to eat and bask in the memories of God's presence and intimacy at the conference. It was like experiencing a little taste of heaven. It was three solid days of worship, testimonies, messages of truth—encompassing the lives of brothers and sisters who have experienced the true power of God's transforming love. What more could you ask for besides heaven?

As the days get darker, it will be harder and harder to stand for truth. The trials and temptations will become more frequent and with a stronger intensity. The Bible tells us that if possible even the elect could be deceived.

> For false messiahs and false prophets will appear and perform great signs and wonders to deceive, if possible, even the elect. (Matthew 24:24 NIV)
>
> But know this, that in the last days perilous times will come: For men will be lovers of themselves, lovers of money, boasters, proud, blasphemers, disobedient to parents, unthankful, unholy, unloving, unforgiving, slanderers, without self-control, brutal, despisers of good, traitors, headstrong, haughty, lovers of pleasure rather than lovers of God, having a form of godliness but denying its power. And from such people turn away! (2 Timothy 3:1–5 NKJV)

Wow, if this doesn't describe our "selfie" culture, I don't know what does. Don't get caught up. Don't let the lure of this world entice you. It all looks so glamorous on the front end but is filled with dead man's bones on the back end. The glory of this world has nothing to offer but death and destruction. Stay close to God, pray continuously, and stay in His Word. He will protect you. He will impart His truth, wisdom, and strength so that you will be able to withstand the tumultuous waves of darkness and deception, standing firm on the rock of truth until Jesus returns.

Although times will be tough, we can rejoice!

> I have told you these things, so that in Me you may have [perfect] peace and confidence. In the world you have tribulation and trials and distress and frustration; but be of good cheer [take courage; be confident, certain, undaunted]! For I have overcome the world. [I have deprived it of power to harm you and have conquered it for you.] (Matthew 16:33, AMP)

Greater is He that is in us than He that is in this world. We can have victory, but it takes effort on our part to obey God and let Him be the driver. Praise Him today for all your blessings! Praise Him today for all your sorrows! Praise Him today for all your trials. Praise Him today for all your hurts, all your loneliness, all your sadness. Ask God to reveal what you can learn through this and to help you see this from a heavenly perspective. Then sit quiet at His feet like Mary, and *wait* for His direction. His direction will be evident and confirmed by His ever-loving peace.

Discussion and Study Guide

Memory Verse

> No temptation has overtaken you except what is common to mankind. And God is faithful; he will not let you be tempted beyond what you can bear. But when you are tempted, he will also provide a way out so that you can endure it. (1 Corinthians 10:13, NIV)

Discussion Questions and Exercises for This Week

What trials are you facing in your life right now?

Are you praying for God to remove them or asking Him to show you what you can learn through them?

What is your plan to get through them? What do you think God's plan is for you to get through them? Which plan are you following? Which plan provides blessing and rewards in the end?

Are you praising God for your trials? How?

Are you bringing certain trials or temptations into the light with someone you can trust?

Are you seeking counsel or looking for a support group? If so, how? Do you need help in finding a group?

What are three ways you can die to self? How will you carry them out this week?

What are some ways you can overcome pride? How will you carry them out this week?

Do you struggle with jealousy and envy? How can you turn those around according to God's Word?

Do you struggle with unforgiveness or hatred toward your enemies? How can you have victory over the bitterness this produces in your soul?

How will you remain in victory this week?

Prayer

Lord Jesus, help me remain in victory through the storms of life. Help me cling to Your Word where all power and strength are derived. Help me seek godly, uplifting friends who delight in You and not the world. Give me wisdom and discernment in each decision. Help me die to self and seek to love others more than myself. Please help me turn around all jealousy and envy to encouragement and praise. Help me to forgive and pray Your blessings on all those who have hurt me or I consider my enemies. Please help me be more humble, uplifting others rather than seeking my own praise, which comes from pride. Help me rest at Your feet daily, waiting for Your confirming peace that provides the guiding light to my victory path.

Daily Readings

Meditate on the verses each day. Take some time to look up any cross-reference verses in the margin and read any commentary in your Bible.

Day 1

Read Matthew 16:24–27.

List a few cross-references here, and pick one for us to read.

Did anything in the commentary stand out to you?

What did you hear?

What do you think?

What will you do?

What is your prayer?

Day 2

Read James 1:2–8.

List a few cross-references here, and pick one for us to read.

Did anything in the commentary stand out to you?

What did you hear?

What do you think?

What will you do?

What is your prayer?

_____

_____

_____

_____

_____

_____

_____

_____

_____

_____

_____

_____

_____

_____

_____

_____

_____

_____

Day 3

Read 2 Timothy 3:1–5.

List a few cross-references here, and pick one for us to read.

Did anything in the commentary stand out to you?

What did you hear?

What do you think?

What will you do?

What is your prayer?

Day 4

Read 2 Corinthians 12:6–10.

List a few cross-references here, and pick one for us to read.

Did anything in the commentary stand out to you?

What did you hear?

What do you think?

What will you do?

What is your prayer?

Day 5

Read 1 Chronicles 29:10–12.

List a few cross-references here, and pick one for us to read.

Did anything in the commentary stand out to you?

What did you hear?

What do you think?

What will you do?

What is your prayer?

WEEK 6

Finding Victory through Thanksgiving, Praise, and Worship

One of the best ways to find strength for every journey is by giving the Lord thanksgiving and praise even during our difficult times. Giving the Lord thanksgiving and praise lifts our spirit and provides a whole new outlook away from the cares of this world and into the presence and intimacy of our all-loving God. Thankfulness puts us in proper alignment with God, whereas grumbling and complaining is a sin and brings us into a state of depression. In Psalm 22:3, it states that God inhabits the praises of his people. I can personally say that during intense worship times, I can feel the strong presence of God unlike any other private time with Him.

> Thou art holy, O thou that inhabits the praise of Israel. (Psalm 22:3)

> Enter his gates with thanksgiving and his courts with praise; give thanks to him and praise his name. For the Lord is good and his love endures forever; his faithfulness continues through all generations. (Psalm 100:4–5)

Praise and worship are very powerful spiritual weapons that lead us into victory. It is impossible to worship and worry at the same time. These are complete opposites. Worry opens the door for Satan, and worship shuts the door in his face. This is an area of warfare that sometimes gets completely overlooked but is one of the most powerful practices that we can incorporate into our daily lives. When we are filled with praise, thanksgiving, and worship, the enemy has no place to sneak in as we are completely immersed in God's presence and protection. When we worry, we are trusting in our own abilities and *not* trusting that God is in complete control of the situation. It all comes down to living a self-centered life versus a God-centered life. However, don't beat yourself up if you worry. This takes time and effort to develop, and we will slip up from time to time as we continue to live in this flesh suit.

Worry can sneak up on us. One moment, we can be in complete peace and enjoyment of our surroundings, and then in an instant, we can be jolted into a state of panic from an unexpected tragedy. This is a natural human reaction that we all go through. However, we have something very powerful inside of us that we can learn how to access in times like these. That power comes from the Holy Spirit, who can interrupt this panic signal and replace it with peace if we can learn and practice how to access this power. As soon as the panic signal is turned on, we need to immediately recognize it and realize that we have a choice on which pathway to let that signal travel. Either we can listen to the Holy Spirit, or we can listen to our own mind. If we decide to listen to the Holy Spirit, then we can immediately say, "I trust You, God, and I release this problem to You." Then God can replace the panic and worry with peace and direct us calmly on what He wants us to do. He may not want us to do anything but trust Him to work it all out. However, He may direct us to take some action, or He may send someone to help.

One thing that we can know for sure is once we release it to God, He can go to work, and we can rest in the fact that He is faithful to fulfill His promises. He promises to never leave us nor forsake us.

> Be strong and courageous. Do not be afraid or terrified because of them, for the LORD your God goes with you; he will never leave you nor forsake you. (Deuteronomy 31:6)

If you are in a state of worry, don't beat yourself up about it. Instead, ask God to help you give it over to Him. Get in His Word, pray with a friend, find your favorite worship CD, and start worshiping and praising God. Look back to all that He has done in your life and start counting your blessings. Then watch your worry start to dissipate as you are filled with the love and power of God through praise and worship. Keep it going until it's gone!

Our memory verse says it all: "Rejoice in the Lord always." I will say it again: *rejoice!* Whenever God repeats something in His Word, it is vital that we pay close attention as these are the treasures that bring abundant blessings. When I learned to thank God for everything, even the little things, He opened up a whole new realm to me. I started noticing Him in every aspect of my life. I noticed how my scheduled flowed so smoothly, how everything in my day was like a puzzle piece that fit perfectly in place. I look back at how He took care of my pool during some challenging healing times. I keep my pool open all year as I believe it is more work to close a pool than to just keep it open. However, during the fall, it is a lot of work to keep clean due to all the trees surrounding it. So during this time, when the Lord was revealing how He is in every aspect of my life, I would come home knowing that I would have a huge job in front of me cleaning out the leaves. Then one day, He gave me such a sweet surprise! I looked up and thanked Him for this tremendous blessings. I came home, and *not one* leaf had fallen into the pool, but they were all around it. *Not one leaf.* That has never happened, and it happened a lot that fall! It was the easiest fall pool maintenance I had ever experienced.

I love how He showed up one summer during a difficult time of transition not having the desire to do much around the house and especially outside around the pool. It was a barren place of old memories that I had abandoned for several years during my time of healing. Around the pool, were all these beautiful flower pots that were all empty. Then to my surprise, I noticed an exotic plant growing up in one of my most beautiful pots. It sparked an excitement in me as I knew this was from God. He put a message in my heart that he was brining me back to life. I would come out each day with anticipation to see the new growth and progress of the beautiful purple blooms. It was so beautiful and looked like something from Hawaii. It was God's way of showing me how much He loved me and that He was with me.

The summer of 2014, He encouraged my Bible study group to have a flower shower for me to fill all the empty pots. I had so many that I stopped counting and really didn't know the exact number. God put it in the hearts of my dear friends to bring all these beautiful plants and flowers. I am so thankful for these friends as they were such a blessing and treasure to me. He even touched the heart of a new friend whom I had only known for several weeks to bring a truckload of plants. She called me while I was on the way home from Bible study to ask me if I was still having the flower shower. I had mentioned it to her briefly and didn't think she was really interested, but God put it in her heart to bring a truckload of plants and flowers. They brought the dirt and everything. I had two favorite large pots that were on each end of the pool. We filled one with a beautiful hibiscus plant with pink flowers. As we finished up, we noticed that we didn't have a plant of similar size for the other large pot and was thinking that another hibiscus plant would be perfect. All of a sudden, we hear someone coming to the fence gate, and I could see through the slats of the fence that they were carrying the same size hibiscus plant. As she walked into the yard with the second hibiscus plant, we noticed it had the same color flowers as well. We all started laughing as we knew this was totally God showing us His amazing glory in this event. How awesome is our God!

As I looked around the yard, I was just taken back by this glorious event and thanked God for His goodness to me. This showed me how He is bringing life back into my sin-laden dead bones, and now I have life in Him. It is such an exciting journey to follow the Lord and let Him lead. Finally, all the pots were filled except one. You may be wondering why He didn't fill all the pots, and I wondered the same thing. At first I thought, *Well, I should go and get a plant to fill the last pot,* but then God said, *I have something very special for that last pot. Just wait on Me.* How cool is that! We can wait on God for *everything* as He wants to show us His glory so that we can brag about Him and let all the glory go to Him. Then what does He do when all the glory goes to Him? He completely fills us with His abundant blessings so that we are lacking nothing as we are in Him.

Therefore, since we are receiving a kingdom that cannot be shaken, let us be thankful, and so worship God acceptably with reverence and awe. (Hebrews 12:28–29)

Discussion and Study Guide

Memory Verse

Rejoice in the Lord always. I will say it again: Rejoice! Let your gentleness be evident to all. The Lord is near. Do not be anxious about anything, but in every situation, by prayer and petition, with thanksgiving, present your requests to God. (Philippians 4:4–6, NIV)

Discussion Questions and Exercises for This Week

Make a list of the top ten blessings that God has done in your life. How do you know they were from God?

What are you thankful for this week?

How can you praise God this week?

What are you doing in your life that brings God all the glory? Do you take the credit, or do you give it over to Him?

What are some of your most memorable worship times with the Lord?

Think back to one of the most profound aha moments from God during an intimate time with Him and share it with the group or someone He directs.

How will you remain in victory this week?

Prayer

Lord Jesus, help me to know You more intimately through praise and worship during the good times and the difficult times. Give me the strength to handle worry in the power of the Holy Spirit at its onset. Open my eyes to the little things You do, and give me a joyful heart as I encounter them. Help me have assurance in Your promises that You are always with me and will never forsake me. Give me a humble heart so that I can thank You for all that I have and everything that happens to me. Help me to seek and follow Your direction in all that I do even if I don't understand it at the time. Help me not to take credit for all the blessings You have given to me but to give You all the honor and glory forever in the name of my precious Lord and Savior, Jesus Christ.

Daily Readings

Meditate on the verses each day. Take some time to look up any cross-reference verses in the margin and read any commentary in your Bible or Bible app.

Day 1

Read Psalm 150.

List a few cross-references here, and pick one that stands out to meditate on and/or share with someone.

Did anything in the commentary stand out to you?

What did you hear?

What do you think?

What will you do?

What is your prayer?

Day 2

Read Psalm 103:1–5.

List a few cross-references here, and pick one that stands out to meditate on and/or share with someone.

Did anything in the commentary stand out to you?

What did you hear?

What do you think?

What will you do?

What is your prayer?

Day 3

Read John 4:23–24.

List a few cross-references here, and pick one that stands out to meditate on and/or share with someone.

Did anything in the commentary stand out to you?

What did you hear?

What do you think?

What will you do?

What is your prayer?

Day 4

Read Psalm 95:1–7.

List a few cross-references here, and pick one that stands out to meditate on and/or share with someone.

Did anything in the commentary stand out to you?

What did you hear?

What do you think?

What will you do?

What is your prayer?

LIVING IN VICTORY

Day 5

Read Colossians 3:14–16.

List a few cross-references here, and pick one that stands out to meditate on and/or share with someone.

Did anything in the commentary stand out to you?

What did you hear?

What do you think?

What will you do?

What is your prayer?

Defeat and Struggle or Victory and Power? You Decide!

God created us with a freewill to choose to have victory in Him or live a defeated Christian life, always struggling. He gave us the will to choose between life and death, and He even gives us the answer in the following passage.

> This day I call the heavens and the earth as witnesses against you that I have set before you life and death, blessings and curses. Now choose life, so that you and your children may live. (Deuteronomy 30:19)

Now choose life! Have you chosen life? Who are you living for? Are you living for yourself, your family, your friends, your career, your ministry, your enjoyment, your popularity, your prestige, your money, or your power? Or have you been able to lay these things on the altar before God, who gave them to you in the first place? Is He the One you can't stop thinking about, the One with whom you talk to and pray to every day, the One you sing to and worship, the One you are thankful to and praise every moment you get? Do you post on social media about Him, or is it all about *you?* What is your motive when you post on social media? I know these are some hard truth questions, but taking the time to examine our hearts and our motives will help us determine the areas we need to confess and release to God so that He can work to move us forward in victory. This message really speaks to my heart as the Holy Spirit is guiding me to write it.

Victory is lost when we have no patience to wait on God!

But they who wait for the LORD shall renew their strength; they shall mount up with wings like eagles; they shall run and not be weary; they shall walk and not faint. (Isaiah 40:31, ESV)

It is so important to spend time with God and follow what the Holy Spirit is telling us. Many of us go about our day in the flesh and don't seek God in everything we do. I don't have time for that. You may say, "Well, God gave us a brain, so we can think and do for ourselves—right?" *No!*

For my thoughts are not your thoughts, neither are your ways my ways, saith the LORD. (Isaiah 55:8)

This is why we get so tired and weary because we are doing everything in our own strength and not being *patient* enough to wait on God and His peace so we can follow the Spirit's leading. We are just in too much of a hurry. Why do you think we are in such a hurry? What is our motive behind the hurry? Asking ourselves these questions with a humble heart may lead us to a revelation about something we need to give up to God so that we can slow down, wait on Him, and receive the amazing peace He has to offer. When we operate in the Spirit, we experience the fruits of the Spirit: love, joy, peace, patience, and self-control. God says, "You will know them by their fruit." If someone is always stressed out and frantic, they are being led by the flesh. Time to slow down and seek God.

> A song of ascents of Solomon. Unless the LORD builds the house, the builders labor in vain. Unless the LORD watches over the city, the guards stand watch in vain. (Psalm 127:1)

If we are not following God's plan (operating in the flesh), we are completely wasting our time. We will not have success. We may even experience the praise of men and receive some earthly "success." However, we know what happens to all our accomplishments that were developed in the flesh (filthy rags)—they get burned up and disappear.

> For no one can lay any foundation other than the one already laid, which is Jesus Christ. If anyone builds on this foundation using gold, silver, costly stones, wood, hay or straw, their work will be shown for what it is, because the Day will bring it to light. It will be revealed with fire, and the fire will test the quality of each person's work. If what has been built survives, the builder will receive a reward. If it is burned up, the builder will suffer loss but yet will be saved—even though only as one escaping through the flames. (1 Corinthians 3:11–15, NIV)

However, when we follow God's plan (operating in the Spirit), we receive complete peace, fulfillment, and a reward that lasts forever. I ask you, why would you want to do it any other way?

I was creating a preliminary marketing plan for a ministry leader, and God revealed something He wanted me to put in the e-mail. He gave me the verse Psalm 127:1: "Unless the Lord builds the house, the builders labor in vain." I started typing the verse in the beginning of the e-mail and was having a hard time with it. I would remove it, and then God would convict me to put it back. I went back and forth with this a few times until I finally put the verse in the e-mail as the number one principle for marketing success. That leader immediately sent a reply e-mail with a picture of her journal with a verse she had just written. Can you guess which verse? God is so amazing when He wants us to do something as He will keep bringing it up until we hopefully obey.

If God is *not* in it, it will fail! If God is not in the center of any ministry, it can become an idol. We must seek Him in every aspect of the ministry to make sure it has His endorsement, which is evidenced by peace. If it does not have His endorsement, it opens the door for the enemy. Ministry leaders must walk in humility and obedience to God's Word, following the Holy Spirit so that the enemy has no open doors to set subtle land mines to destroy the ministry. There is nothing the enemy wants more then to destroy ministries and divide believers. God empowers us with many amazing gifts. We each operate in different gifts of the Spirit such as the gift of knowledge, healing, prophecy, and the discernment of spirits. I believe the gift of discernment is vital for ministry leaders and if they don't have it to recognize the fact and to pray for someone who does to become their board chair. The board chair should then use that gift to select and vet all other board members, ministry staff, and volunteers to make sure there are *no open* doors for the enemy to attack the ministry. We must be alert in these times in order to remain in victory! As the Bible tells us, many will fall away during the end times (Matthew 24:10).

Why do many Christians live defeated lives? It seems that today most of the messages are on struggle. And yes, God says we will have trouble in this world, but He also says we can have victory though Jesus and the power of the resurrection that is inside of us. So choosing life or death—we choose to pull verses out of context to fit our needs that keep us in defeat, or we choose to focus on the verses that build up our faith and teach us to walk by faith and in the power of the Holy Spirit.

Obstacles That Keep Us from Having Victory

But mark this: There will be terrible times in the last days. People will be lovers of themselves, lovers of money, boastful, proud, abusive, disobedient to their parents, ungrateful, unholy, without love, unforgiving, slanderous, without self-control, brutal, not lovers of the good, treacherous, rash, conceited, lovers of pleasure rather than lovers of God—having a form of godliness but denying its power. Have nothing to do with such people. (2 Timothy 3:1–5)

So this verse pretty much lays out what we are seeing in the church today.

God has put on my heart five key areas that I believe are keeping the church in defeat and in constant struggle.

1. **Obedience to God's Word**. I believe this is the number one reason we are not seeing victory in the church today. We are following our own path (self-centered) and not

following God's plan (God-centered). Many churches are caught up in this feel-good emotionalism and "getting into the presence," being on guard with these churches, especially if they pay more attention to the experiences than they do the Word of God. The power of God manifests in our lives when we *repent* of our sin, when we are obedient and surrender our lives to the Word of God and the promptings of the Holy Spirit, not when we conjure up an atmosphere with smoke machines, lights, and mesmerizing music with half the church living in blatant sin because it is never addressed in the pulpit. We are to test the spirits to see if they are of God! So that means we need to be rooted and grounded in the Word to have the discernment to know if we are following the Holy Spirit or a deceiving spirit which the Bible tells us will be prevalent in the end-times.

2. **Pride, lovers of self, envy, and jealousy**. Do you consider yourself better than anyone? When you are out in public, do you consider yourself higher than a waitress, a maid, or even the janitor that cleans your office? God dealt with me on this issue by giving me this thought. I am *no* better than the homeless person on the street. I could walk across the street and get hit by a car and be completely debilitated in an instant. We must be kind to everyone as each of us is unique in God's sight. We are all different and made for different purposes in God's kingdom. We are all in different places in our walk with God, so *our job* is to love others as ourselves—actually, more than ourselves (Philippians 2:3). When we can do this, it opens up a whole new realm of God's blessings and shuts the door on the enemy.

3. **Lovers of pleasure rather than lovers of God**. How much time does God get in our schedule compared to sports activities, entertainment, and even vacations? Do you take a vacation with God? How about fasting and prayer? How much time does that get in the schedule? This is an eye-opener to where our real priorities lie and in whom we are really delighting—the world and pleasure or the Word and God?

4. **Unforgiveness**. This is the single most popular poison the enemy uses against God's people to keep us in defeat and struggle. Who are you mad at right now? Who makes you angry every time you think about them and what they did or said to you? The enemy loves to fill our heads with negative thoughts about others because this keeps us defeated, *and* God says He then cannot forgive us! This is something that I really struggle with and have to constantly give over to God. I try to take action immediately by taking my thoughts captive, praising, and thinking on God. Eventually, God gives me the power to turn those thoughts into love. I ask Him to help me see that person the way He sees them and to love them the way He loves them. This has been a winning prayer for me. However, this is something I must exercise daily to overcome this particular struggle and turn it into victory.

5. **Idolatry** (sports, entertainment, people, money, material things, etc.). If we stop and think about what we think about more than God, and seek Him to show us our idols, I am sure that He will reveal them. Then we can seek God for help and guidance to put Him first.

It Is Time for God's People to Wake Up!

If my people, who are called by my name, will humble themselves and pray and seek my face and turn from their wicked ways, then I will hear from heaven, and I will forgive their sin and will heal their land. (2 Chronicles 7:14 NIV)

This verse is for God's people, *not* unbelievers. We have to get with God and seek Him *first* in our lives, or we will keep floating down the river of defeat and struggle.

I can so relate to Joyce Meyer when she states that she could not be a counselor because she doesn't understand how Christians can live in defeat for very long when they have the life-giving power of the Holy Spirit inside of them, who will counsel them in God's Word. She certainly has room to talk since she came out of a very abusive background but was able to overcome by following God's truth.

But the Comforter (Counselor, Helper, Intercessor, Advocate, Strengthener, Standby), the Holy Spirit, Whom the Father will send in My name [in My place, to represent Me and act on My behalf], He will teach you all things. And He will cause you to recall (will remind you of, bring to your remembrance) everything I have told you. (John 14:26 AMP)

The Bible speaks about the great falling away or the apostasy that will occur in the end-times. He says that the sign of the times will be that the church will fall away. During my first three years in the healing process, I did not hear many preachers or speakers talk about victory. The main narrative was about the struggle and how grace is all we need.

What shall we say, then? Shall we go on sinning so that grace may increase? By no means! We are those who have died to sin; how can we live in it any longer? (Romans 6:1 NIV)

For our struggle is not against flesh and blood, but against the rulers, against the authorities, against the powers of this dark world and against the spiritual forces of evil in the heavenly realms. (Ephesians 6:12 NIV)

The word *struggle* in this passage is the Greek word *pale*. It is a wrestling term ("a contest between two to throw the other to the ground and hold him there; to hold him down with his hand upon his neck"). Do you think this could be why so many of those who profess to be Christians struggle and feel held down and "choked" by the enemy?

How do we have power to overcome our struggles?

I have given you authority to trample on snakes and scorpions and to overcome all the power of the enemy; nothing will harm you. (Luke 10:19 NIV)

I love one of Joyce Meyer's sayings: "You can't be pitiful and powerful at the same time! Need to pick one and go with it."

We can decide to live in constant defeat and struggle, or we can decide to live a powerful, victorious life by receiving and living in God's power through the Holy Spirit. However, we must be in *obedience* to God's Word. If we are not living in obedience, we will not have access to the power of the Holy Spirit. If we are delighting in the world and its messages, then we are opening doors for Satan and allowing him to have at least partial control of our lives. It all comes down to which "father" you are serving—or to say it another way, what are you delighting in? The enemy/world or God/Word? What are you feeding, the flesh or the spirit? What messages are you allowing to feed your brain? We all know too well what the world's (secular) messages have to say. Do you watch secular movies or Christian movies? Listening to secular music or Christian music?

I am getting so *tired* of the downtrodden message of struggle. I go to conferences and support groups, and we all sit around and talk about our struggles. We all come back next week and talk about our struggles again. Where are the Christians who are living in victory and talking about the blessings of God and the power they are experiencing in the Holy Spirit? Unfortunately, there are very few; but when you do find one, it is a blessing from heaven. Don't get me wrong, it is vital to be in community with other strong believers to get healing from our hurts and strongholds but at some point, we need to see healing and victory over those issues. I am so convinced we are living in the end-times. No one knows the exact time, but He gives us clues of when we should start looking up. Lift up your heads because your redemption is drawing near (Luke 21:28).

Let no one in any way deceive you, for it will not come unless the apostasy comes first, and the man of lawlessness is revealed, the son of destruction. (2 Thessalonians 2:3 NASB)

The thief comes only to steal and kill and destroy; I came that they may have life, and have it abundantly. (John 10:10 ESV)

He did not come and die for us to live in constant defeat and struggle. He came so we can have life and have it abundantly. He came so that we can know Him and receive the fruit of His Spirit of love, joy, peace, mercy, and goodness. He came so that we can have the power of the resurrection, the faith that moves mountains. He gave the *armor* to *put on* for complete victory over the enemy who is the "father" of this world.

God could have created a bunch of robots to obey His every Word, but He didn't. He wants us to choose to love Him. He wants us to choose to serve Him. So the choice is all ours! Live a defeated, struggling life or a victorious, powerful life in Christ. Time is getting short, and only what is done for Christ (in the Spirit) will last and be rewarded. Which life do you want to live? The choice is all yours and mine!

When the clouds are rolled back and our Redeemer appears oh what a day of rejoicing it will be! And when we hear these words—Well done, My good and faithful servant, The Victory is Won!

Discussion and Study Guide

Memory Verse

But I say unto you, Love your enemies, bless them that curse you, do good to them that hate you, and pray for them which despitefully use you, and persecute you. (Matthew 5:44 KJV)

You may ask why is *this* our memory verse for a week taking about victory over struggle. Because I believe this verse is the most difficult for a believer to live. And when you humble yourself before God and love Him (do what He says), you will experience the peace and power of God in your life like never before.

Discussion Questions and Exercises for This Week

What is keeping you from victory? Look at the top five areas that God placed on my heart to reveal in this lesson. Do any of these speak to you? Which ones do you need to deal with? Why not deal with them today and decide to live a life of victory? Take some time to pray right now, and ask God to reveal what He wants you to work on first. Then ask Him to help you.

Who do you need to forgive?

Who do you need to love greater than yourself?

What or who gets priority in your life?

Are you feeding your flesh or your spirit? Name the daily activities that feed the spirit. What is the percentage compared to activities that feed your flesh?

When the clouds are rolled back and our Redeemer appears, will you greet Him with expectation or with shame? How much do you long to hear, Well done, My good and faithful servant?

Are you fulfilling the purpose and plan He has for you?

How will you remain in victory this week?

Prayer

Lord Jesus, help me to lay my entire life down on the altar before You. Show me, Lord, the areas that I need to work on to get closer to You and put You first in my life. Forgive me for the sin in my life and help me to abstain from that sin. Open my spiritual eyes to see any open doors into worldly messages that feed my flesh and allow the enemy access. Help me, Lord, to shut those doors by starving the flesh and feeding the Spirit in all areas of my life. Give me wisdom from Your Word and the strength from Your Spirit to understand Your ways and to live in victory by loving You and loving others.

Daily Readings

Meditate on the verses each day. Take some time to look up any cross-reference verses in the margin and read any commentary in your Bible.

Day 1

Read Matthew 5:44.

Please write this verse down, and memorize it because you're going to need it to stay in victory.

List a few cross-references here, and pick one that stands out to meditate on and/or share with someone.

Did anything in the commentary stand out to you?

What did you hear?

What do you think?

What will you do?

What is your prayer?

Day 2

Read Galatians 5:13–26.

List a few cross-references here, and pick one that stands out to meditate on and/or share with someone.

Did anything in the commentary stand out to you?

What did you hear?

What do you think?

What will you do?

What is your prayer?

_____

_____

_____

_____

_____

_____

_____

_____

_____

_____

_____

_____

_____

_____

_____

_____

_____

_____

Day 3

Read Ephesians 5.

List a few cross-references here, and pick one that stands out to meditate on and/or share with someone.

Did anything in the commentary stand out to you?

What did you hear?

What do you think?

What will you do?

What is your prayer?

_____

_____

_____

_____

_____

_____

_____

_____

_____

_____

_____

_____

_____

_____

_____

_____

_____

Day 4

Read John 10:10.

Write this verse here:

List a few cross-references here, and pick one that stands out to meditate on and/or share with someone.

Did anything in the commentary stand out to you?

What did you hear?

What do you think?

What will you do?

What is your prayer?

Day 5

Read 2 Timothy 4:6–8.

List a few cross-references here, and pick one that stands out to meditate on and/or share with someone.

Did anything in the commentary stand out to you?

What did you hear?

What do you think?

What will you do?

What is your prayer?

LIVING IN VICTORY

A PAYER FOR THOSE WHO STRUGGLE
WITH SEXUAL IDENTITY

A prayer for my brother and sisters who struggle with sexual identity issues. This prayer comes from a heart of love as I can totally relate to the struggle.

My heart is heavy as I pray this prayer as one of my brothers has fallen and I want him to know that this prayer comes out of my *love* for him. God loves us all, and I believe He will give those who have fallen away a defining moment, just like He did for me, to choose between *life* or *death*, and I pray this prayer is the catalyst to help you choose...*life—victory* in Christ.

Dear Lord, I come to You with a heavy heart for those who struggle with their sexual identity. I pray Lord that the moment this prayer is read that You bring forth a wind from heaven and pour out Your Spirit to fill hearts and minds with Your truth, love, and grace. Awaken souls and open spiritual eyes as You did for me that night in the bar and let the reader see the true face of what and who they believe is fulfilling their need for intimacy. Remove the veil of deception, dear Lord, and reveal what lurks behind it all. The spirit of seduction, rejection, and rebellion from the front lines of evil.

Give them the strength, Lord, to take that one simple step of faith by raising their hand, letting go of their pride, and asking for help no matter how difficult it may seem. Let them know that once this act of obedience and surrender takes place, that You will usher in the power of heaven to do all the heavy lifting.

Give the reader an insatiable desire to read Your Word and give You priority in their day as You will then pour out Your living water of healing and wholeness and fill them with Your goodness, peace, and overflowing *joy*. I pray for wisdom, discernment, and new sight to bring forth a knowing and understanding from the depth of their soul to their true purpose and belonging that originates from the Creator and not the creature.

Let their true identity now be seen in the reflection of Jesus Christ and in His body of believers.

A Victory Prayer

I pray the Ephesians prayer (Ephesians 3:14–21) over you this day…

For this reason, I kneel before the Father, from whom every family in heaven and on earth derives its name. I pray that out of His glorious riches, He may strengthen you with power through His Spirit in your inner being so that Christ may dwell in your hearts through faith. And I pray that you, being rooted and established in love, may have power, together with all the Lord's holy people, to grasp how wide and long and high and deep is the love of Christ and to know this love that surpasses knowledge—that you may be filled to the measure of all the fullness of God.

Now to Him who is able to do immeasurably more than all we ask or imagine, according to His power that is at work within us, to Him be glory in the church and in Christ Jesus throughout all generations, forever and ever! Amen.

ABOUT THE AUTHOR

Christel Novella is first and foremost a lover of Jesus Christ and the daughter of the Most High King. In Christel's mind, we need not go any further.

The Lord has gifted Christel with a passion for the creative arts and media. It all started in high school in her creative arts classes where she would discover her passion for drawing, painting, and pottery. Christel first realized her gift in this area as selected pieces where displayed in the art department's showcase.

Christel was encouraged by her family to attend nursing school and received a BS in nursing in 1991. Christel loved working in the Neonatal and Adult ICUs. However, the creative passion would surface as Christel would spend all of her time off learning photography, graphic design, and website development online through the Adobe Suite of products then known as Macromedia.

In 2007, she started a media company called Novanet Profits where she serviced many different clients from software companies, website companies, chiropractors, counselors, hair salons, boutiques, construction companies, churches, and ministries. Her services included graphic design, website development, SEO, video production and editing, and social media and mobile marketing strategies.

Then in 2011, God called Christel out of a lifestyle of homosexuality into His glorious light where she would find a home church and a community of believers that would become a strong support system to her growth in the Lord. Here, she would discover her desire and calling to use her media gifts for the Lord where she would provide social media strategy, photography, and video services. She would also volunteer in the church's production department working cameras, ProPresenter, CG, and teleprompter.

As this book is being written, God is calling Christel on a new mission with a fresh new look into the future of online media. This new mission has taken on a new look, a new location with a new name, Kingdom Media Studios.

Kingdom Media Studios is a God-given dream that came to Christel one day during the beginning of her transformation. It was so *big* that she experienced such a download of the plans that she could hardly breathe or stay standing when she heard the Lord say, "One million souls." The plans are extensive and *huge*, and Christel realizes that what the Lord showed her that day can only come from Him. So looking back at how the Lord has worked in her life, she waits once again for Him to open the door and she will walk into it and let Him do all the heavy lifting so that He can receive *all* the glory. Please pray for Christel and KMS as she waits on God to lead and guide her through each phase on this new journey. If you would like to follow Christel and the KMS journey, you can follow on Instagram @kindgom_media_studios on Facebook and subscribe to the newsletter at www.KingdomMediaStudios.com.

CPSIA information can be obtained
at www.ICGtesting.com
Printed in the USA
LVHW050945061020
668075LV00010B/445